North Korean Decisionmaking

Economic Opening, Conventional Deterrence Breakdown, and Nuclear Use

JOHN V. PARACHINI, SCOTT W. HAROLD, GIAN GENTILE,
DEREK GROSSMAN, LEAH HEEJIN KIM, LOGAN MA,
MICHAEL J. MAZARR, LINDA ROBINSON

Prepared for the National Intelligence Council
Approved for public release; distribution unlimited

RAND NATIONAL DEFENSE RESEARCH INSTITUTE

For more information on this publication, visit www.rand.org/t/RRA165-1

Library of Congress Cataloging-in-Publication Data is available for this publication.
ISBN: 978-1-9774-0553-1

Published by the RAND Corporation, Santa Monica, Calif.

Preface

Discerning the decisionmaking of Kim Jong-Un and the North Korean regime on issues of peaceful engagement and warlike actions endures as a mighty challenge for U.S. intelligence analysts and policymakers. In this report, we seek to inform analysis of Democratic People's Republic of Korea (DPRK) leadership decisionmaking. To do so, we use three discussion papers that were written to facilitate discussion of an interagency working group. The three papers are assembled here in a single report. The first discussion paper describes decisionmaking among different authoritarian regimes, including North Korea, and the opening up of those economies to outside engagement. The second paper outlines two different scenarios that might occur when conventional deterrence on the Korean Peninsula breaks down and the resulting decisions that North Korea's leadership could face. The third paper assesses DPRK decisionmaking about nuclear weapon use. The report concludes with some observations, drawn from the issues covered in these three discussion papers, about DPRK decisionmaking and stability on the Korean Peninsula.

This research was sponsored by National Intelligence Council and conducted within the Cyber and Intelligence Policy Center of the RAND National Security Research Division (NSRD), which operates the National Defense Research Institute (NDRI), a federally funded research and development center sponsored by the Office of the Secretary of Defense, the Joint Staff, the Unified Combatant Commands, the Navy, the Marine Corps, the defense agencies, and the defense intelligence enterprise.

For more information on the RAND Cyber and Intelligence Policy Center, see www.rand.org/nsrd/intel or contact the director (contact information is provided on the webpage).

Contents

Tables

Summary

Discerning the decisionmaking of Kim Jong-Un and the North Korean regime on issues of peaceful engagement and warlike actions endures as a mighty challenge for U.S. intelligence analysts and policymakers. The National Intelligence Council requested that the RAND Corporation prepare a series of background papers to facilitate discussion at three Intelligence Community working group meetings on Democratic People's Republic of Korea (DPRK) decisionmaking. The first session focused on the experiences of authoritarian countries and how they navigated toward opening their economies and political systems—more the former than the latter. The second session focused on how conventional deterrence might fail on the Korean Peninsula and how conflict might escalate. The third and final session focused on how nuclear deterrence might break down and nuclear use might ensue.

Insights from Three Discussion Papers

Prospects That North Korea Will Engage in Market Reform

To understand why Kim Jong-Un might decide to adopt a new economic model (and some of the challenges that might result from such a decision), we analyzed the economic opening decisions and experiences of North Korea and three other communist regimes—China, Vietnam, and Cuba—and examined the factors that shaped North Korea's own past reform initiatives.

We concluded that, although no single factor emerges as the sole predictor of a communist regime's decision to open up, several common considerations do appear across the cases studied (Table S.1).

These factors include a rapid deterioration in central government finances; a relaxation in the necessity for ideological purity (linked, in the cases of Vietnam and Cuba, to China's desire to pursue economic liberalization and to the collapse of the Soviet Union, respectively, thus providing Hanoi and Havana with measures of political cover); and, most important, the removal from office or death of key leaders who had opposed reform. Other factors also affect reform decisions; depending on the case, these can be incipient famine and widespread demands for improvement in living conditions that threaten to shake the regime's grip on power, spreading corruption and the erosion of control over the state-led sector of the economy, and/or the loss of a great-power patron.

U.S. policies in encouraging these regimes to open up or sanctioning them for their foreign policies or domestic abuses (carrots or sticks) do not appear to have figured directly in most of these instances of communist reform decisionmaking. Most of these governments were under some degree of economic pressure from the United States and continued to have challenging relationships with

Table S.1
Factors Shaping Communist Economic Reform Initiative Decisions

Factor	China	Vietnam	Cuba	North Korea
Removal of leader opposed to opening	X	X	X	
Scarcity of food and consumer goods	X	X	X	X
Hyperinflation		X		
Loss of foreign aid and patronage		X	X	X
Economic sanctions		X	X	X
Expansion of illicit markets		X		X
Declining central government finances	X	X	X	X
Loosening ideology	X	X	X	

Washington, but their decisions to reform do not appear to be a direct outgrowth of either U.S. threats to impose harsher sanctions or U.S. offers of assistance if the regimes move toward economic liberalization. This suggests that the effects of such incentives are likely to be felt somewhat indirectly and to work only if the Kim regime perceives that it is facing a situation in which U.S.-led sanctions are putting the regime's survival at risk.

Conventional Deterrence on the Korean Peninsula: Two Scenarios for Analysis

What factors affect DPRK thinking and decisionmaking about conventional deterrence and escalation on the Korean Peninsula? We explored this question by selecting and then examining two "what if" scenarios in the year 2022 that depict situations in which conventional deterrence erodes and fails. The scenarios were designed to explore the critical factors that could affect the thinking of the DPRK regime during an evolving crisis and what might lead the regime to attack Republic of Korea (ROK) and U.S. forces stationed on the Peninsula.

The two scenarios posit that a perception of weakened U.S.-ROK deterrence—real or misperceived—by North Korea will lead to erosion of conventional deterrence. Each scenario ends with North Korea carrying out military action, but neither considers the next steps that might occur. The purpose of ending the scenarios in this way was to generate discussion about what happens when a crisis occurs in which conventional military power is used, conventional deterrence erodes, and escalation to the potential use of nuclear weapons becomes a possibility.

An important insight from these two scenarios is that conventional deterrence (which has been effective since 1953) could quickly erode during a crisis, depending on other factors that influence the integrity of deterrence on the Korean Peninsula. Assessing some plausible scenarios in which conventional deterrence is stressed on the Peninsula shows how a stable alignment can be upset by conventional conflict in response to a crisis and quickly escalate to a nuclear crisis. Once fighting with conventional weapons begins, there might be few off-ramps for avoiding a nuclear exchange. Thus, understanding how conventional deterrence works—and how it might fail—is important to understanding nuclear deterrence.

North Korea Nuclear Doctrine

This case study evaluates questions about North Korea's approach to nuclear weapons, such as how North Korea thinks about (1) its nuclear doctrine, desired force posture, and related capabilities needs; (2) the relationship between its nuclear and conventional forces; and (3) the role of nuclear weapons in deterrence and escalation. It also evaluates the conditions under which North Korea might consider nuclear use.

This case study evaluates these key questions by examining open-source data on possible DPRK nuclear doctrines and comparing them with scenarios that might call for the use of nuclear weapons. The result is necessarily somewhat speculative, both because our knowledge of North Korea's nuclear doctrine is extremely limited and because the actual response of national leaders in any given contingency cannot be predicted.

The evaluation identified five potential doctrines—minimum deterrence, catalytic, massive preemption, assured retaliation, and asymmetric escalation—and assessed the possible utility of different nuclear doctrines to North Korea in terms of three specific regime objectives for its nuclear force (not necessarily in priority order):

1. bolstering regime strength through prestige, legitimacy, coercive power, and nationalist credibility
2. deterring U.S. coercion or attack
3. in extreme circumstances, supporting offensive operations through escalation dominance, empowering provocation, or offensive warfare.

Evolving DPRK nuclear doctrine and capabilities point to potential cases in which North Korea might use nuclear weapons. The interplay among doctrine, capabilities, and weapons use is outlined in Table S.2.

An important insight revealed in this roster of nuclear use scenarios is that the United States and South Korea have a significant ability

Table S.2
Scenarios for DPRK Nuclear Use

Scenario	Forcing Conditions	Form of Nuclear Use
1: Limited strike to interrupt U.S.-ROK military operations	Conventional fighting underway; U.S.-ROK forces operating inside North Korea or on verge of doing so; no fatal threat to regime yet	Single nuclear warhead or small number of them used against lead elements of advancing U.S.-ROK forces
2: Large-scale strike against U.S. force flow and military targets	Conflict might be underway or not yet begun; North Korea perceives that United States is beginning process of large-scale attack to end regime	Dozens of nuclear weapons (the entire DPRK force minus perhaps a handful of strategic-deterrent warheads) used against U.S. military facilities and forces; possibly other targets, such as ROK and Japanese facilities
3: Ultimate deterrent strike against U.S. targets	In endgame, North Korea employs whatever weapons can reach the territorial United States to punish or paralyze U.S. military action	Small number of ICBM or SLBM weapons targeted against territorial United States
4: Nuclear coercive threats and potential first strike against South Korea to compel surrender	U.S.-ROK alliance has fractured, China unwilling to prevent outcome, North Korea sees chance to realize its ultimate goal	Unclear; if coercive threat was rejected, could involve a graduated campaign of nuclear use

NOTE: ICBM = intercontinental ballistic missile; SLBM = submarine-launched ballistic missile.

to control the circumstances that would lead North Korea to undertake nuclear use. The first three scenarios would all stem from a DPRK perception of regime threat and (in some cases) would require the initiation of conflict. The fourth scenario can be forestalled with continuing alliance commitments and coordination with other key actors, such as China. Through a combination of restraint, political agreements to reduce mutual threat perceptions and the perceived risk of war, and continued credible deterrent threats, the United States should be able have significant confidence in its ability to mitigate the scenarios for DPRK nuclear use.

Conclusions

In April 2019, North Korea set an end-of-year deadline to move U.S.-DPRK negotiations forward; in a New Year's speech that December, Kim Jong-Un argued that it was up to the United States to make accommodations or his country would end its self-imposed restraint on nuclear and missile testing. He indicated that the world would see a new strategic weapon in the country's arsenal. U.S. officials and North Korea watchers wondered whether North Korea would conduct a nuclear test or test another ballistic missile that could reach the United States. In the end Kim did not test a weapon system, but he did state that (1) his country would go a new way and not abandon its nuclear weapons capabilities while waiting for the United States to (in Kim's view) negotiate constructively and (2) he would work with other countries to achieve his country's safety and prosperity.

Kim Jong-Un's New Year's message did not shock the world with any new threatening revelation.[1] Rather, he indicated that the struggle to protect North Korea as a sovereign state would continue unabated and that the way ahead would be difficult. The country will continue to modernize its defense capabilities and pursue economic advancement at the same time. Through international diplomacy in 2019 with several major powers—most importantly the United States and China but also Russia—Kim sought to demonstrate that North Korea is a sovereign state with relations that protect it by virtue of its multinational connections.

Although the Kim regime labors under international sanctions, it receives enough resources and funding from sanctions evasion activities that it can pursue limited showcase economic projects in tourist resorts and add to its military capabilities at the same time. The showcase projects in special economic zones can help keep the elite cadre economically satisfied. Similarly, having already achieved a credible conventional and nuclear deterrent posture, North Korea can continue

---

[1] Report of the Fifth Plenary Meeting of the 7th Central Committee of the WPK (Kim Jong Un's 2020 New Year Address), as published and translated into English by the Korean Central News Agency, National Committee of North Korea, January 1, 2020.

its weapon modernization plans at a level that does not spark additional international pressure.

Thus, the stability on the Korean Peninsula can withstand periodic shocks. Unless there is a bolt out of the blue, there is little danger of stability eroding quickly. Kim Jong-Un and the North Korean leadership perceive DPRK nuclear weapons capability as essential to safeguarding the regime's survival. Only a threat to the regime's survival would lead it to the existential decision of using a nuclear weapon and risk a massive retaliatory strike. North Korean leaders perceive their nuclear capability as the ultimate guarantee of their survival. If accidents that trigger war can be avoided, North Korea, South Korea, and the United States have options for limiting the risk of putting the North Korean leadership in a position where it believes it faces an existential choice that lacks clear or desirable endpoints. Monitoring the evolution of the North Korean leadership decision options will be a critical task for the U.S. Intelligence Community to provide U.S. policymakers with decision advantage.

Acknowledgments

Project leaders John V. Parachini and Scott Harold thank the colleagues who prepared the discussion papers. Linda Robinson drew on her extensive experience to write the section on Cuba. Derek Grossman prepared the section on Vietnam. Logan Ma prepared the section on China. Heejin Kim prepared the section on North Korea. Gian Gentile prepared the material in the second chapter outlining plausible scenarios depicting the breakdown of conventional deterrence on the Korean Peninsula. Finally, Michael Mazarr prepared the chapter on what might be North Korea's nuclear doctrine.

Additional thanks go to the National Intelligence Council project sponsors and their interagency collaborators for drawing on the materials contained in this report to examine the dimensions of DPRK decisionmaking on different topics that have current value and long-term implications. These individuals have a daunting challenge to help the President and other senior U.S. leaders make decisions on how to engage with North Korea leaders, and they do so with very imperfect information. Thus, looking to historical case studies, plausible scenarios, and systematic outlines of options are worthy approaches to a set of issues with profound implications for stability on the Korean Peninsula.

Finally, our team thanks Larry Harrison and Soo Kim for their thoughtful peer review comments, Paul Steinberg for his careful review and suggestions for improvement, and Liam McLane for reviewing citations and helping compile the reference section of the report.

Abbreviations

C2	command and control
CFC	Combined Forces Command
DMZ	demilitarized zone
DPRK	Democratic People's Republic of Korea
FDI	foreign direct investment
GDP	gross domestic product
KCNA	Korean Central News Agency
ICBM	intercontinental ballistic missiles
ROK	Republic of Korea
SEZ	special economic zone
SLBM	submarine-launched ballistic missile
SOE	state-owned enterprise
SRV	Socialist Republic of Vietnam
UNC	United Nations Command
VCP	Vietnamese Communist Party

CHAPTER ONE

Introduction

On February 27 and 28, 2019, the North Korea–United States Hanoi Summit (commonly known as the Hanoi Summit) took place in Vietnam; it followed the Singapore Summit in June 2018 between the leaders from the United States and North Korea. The Hanoi Summit was truncated and no agreement was reached. President Donald Trump's administration argued that the summit was abruptly ended when North Korea demanded an end to all sanctions against it; the North Koreans argued that they were only asking for a partial lifting of the five United Nations sanctions imposed on the country between 2016 and 2017.

With talks between the United States and North Korea at a standstill, U.S. policymakers must consider what the Democratic People's Republic of Korea (DPRK) regime might do moving forward and know what signs or decisions to look for. At the request of the National Intelligence Council, we prepared a series of background papers (drawing on previous work and reviewing relevant literature) to help facilitate discussion for three Council working group sessions.

The first session focused on the experience of authoritarian countries and how they navigated toward opening their economies and political systems—more the former than the latter. The second session focused on how conventional deterrence might fail on the Korean Peninsula and how conflict might escalate. The third and final session focused on how nuclear deterrence might break down and nuclear use might ensue.

The paper we created for the first session (Chapter Two) addressed whether North Korean leader Kim Jong-Un would or could pursue a China or Vietnam model of economic liberalization, which is something the Trump administration has hoped for. The second paper (Chapter Three) covered the stability of conventional deterrence on the Korean Peninsula, how mistakes might occur, and the severity of consequences for miscommunication. The third paper (Chapter Four) focused on nuclear deterrence; although such deterrence seems stable now, it could change as the DPRK arsenal grows. That said, the United States has considerable influence on how to maintain the nuclear deterrent relationship. This report concludes with some observations, drawn from the issues covered in these three discussion papers, about DPRK decisionmaking and stability on the Korean Peninsula.

CHAPTER TWO

Prospects That North Korea Will Engage in Market Reform

Will Kim open up the DPRK economy? The United States and South Korea have sought to encourage Pyongyang to make a strategic decision to abandon its nuclear weapon and ballistic missile programs, adopt a new relationship with the international community, and chart a path to economic development premised on markets, trade, and foreign direct investment (FDI) in North Korea. Kim has indicated that the policy priorities of his administration are now shifting toward economic development, and he joined the Singapore Summit statement pledging "firm and unwavering commitment to complete denuclearization of the Korean Peninsula."[1] North Korea has often hinted at both these goals in the past without actually following through. If North Korea were to pursue a strategic decision to reform its economic model and open up to the outside world, what factors would likely lead it to do so and what indicators would there be that the regime was serious this time?

To shed light on these questions, we reviewed the opening and reform decisions of North Korea and three other communist regimes—China, Vietnam, and Cuba—and the history of North Korea's own economic initiatives. We looked for commonalities and differences across the cases to determine what factors appear to correlate with a regime deciding to open up to the outside world. In the cases studies on China, Vietnam, and Cuba, we sought to highlight the internal debates in those countries over whether, why, and how to reform and

[1] Donald J. Trump and Kim Jong-Un, joint statement, Singapore Summit, June 12, 2018.

the factors that spurred decisionmakers to move in a particular direction. Our research drew on open, secondary source literature, some primary source Communist Party or government documents, and some interviews. This analysis is intended to help provide a framework for thinking through the relationship between political decisionmaking and economic reform.

In this chapter, we start by looking at the key factors that we determined affected the decisionmaking of the countries examined. We then examine the reform decisions of China, Vietnam, Cuba, and North Korea from approximately the 1980s through the present.

First, we lay out the experience of Deng Xiaoping in reforming China after the death of Mao Zedong, from 1978 to roughly 1992. We highlight key differences between the China and North Korea cases, such as the much more collective Chinese approach to decisionmaking, the declining role of ideology, and the greater confidence of Chinese leaders that their regime could survive opening up.

Second, we examine the case of the Vietnamese Communist Party (VCP) leadership following the death of Party General Secretary Le Duan and the VCP's 1986 decision to pursue *doi moi* ("renovation" or economic reform) to stave off inflation, famine, and possible economic and state collapse.

Third, we then shift away from Asian communist regimes to describe the experiences of the regimes of Fidel Castro and Raúl Castro Ruz in Cuba, which might be the case that is most comparable to North Korea today. Like North Korea but unlike China and Vietnam, Cuba was a dynastic communist regime for more than 50 years, with founding leader Fidel Castro and his brother Raúl refusing to relax the ideological strictures on the economy, even given massive hunger for goods and food among the Cuban people and the loss of a superpower patron in the Soviet Union. Most Cuban economic reforms have been piecemeal and, to date, have resulted in a far less open economic system than those of China or Vietnam (which themselves remain far from truly market-based); instead, the regime has been willing to reform only reluctantly, and when confronted with a choice between survival or ideological purity.

Fourth, we explore North Korea's similar experience of losing great-power patronage, the regime's shift to extorting aid and assistance from the international community and its immediate neighbors (and through illicit activities), and the extent to which it has sought to reimpose control over the economic life of the country whenever it has had the breathing room to try to do so.

Finally, we offer some concluding thoughts on the takeaway lessons from these cases for the analysis of North Korea's likeliest next steps and decisionmaking process.

Factors That Influence Economic Reform Decisionmaking

We compiled a series of eight factors that we hypothesized might shape leadership decisionmaking of communist regimes on economic reforms:

- removal of leader opposed to opening up the country
- scarcity of food and consumer goods in the country
- existence of hyperinflation
- loss of foreign aid and patronage
- economic sanctions imposed on the country
- expansion of illicit markets in the country
- decline of central government finances
- loosening of the country's overarching ideology.

We then sought to test the validity of our hypothesis with a set of case studies. Not all factors applied equally to the case studies, but all were present to some degree.

Factors That Influenced China's Economic Reform Decisions

China's economic reform is the archetype of a country transitioning from a Soviet-style planned economy to a market-based one. The decades following the Third Plenary Session of the Eleventh Central Committee in 1978 saw an unprecedented period of economic growth, resulting in the country's transformation into a global economic powerhouse. Many analysts, including many Chinese observers, suggest that North Korea could take steps toward economic liberalization that would enable it to follow a similar path. Thus, China's experiences could serve as a blueprint for DPRK economic reform. Here, we chart the course of the Chinese transition and highlight the motivations, goals, pitfalls, and zigzags in China's economic reform and opening up. The first section lays a foundation for the following sections by describing China's situation on the eve of economic reform in 1978. The second section provides an overview of the key debates and issues that emerged in China's economic reforms. The final section compares and contrasts China at the onset of the economic reforms with North Korea today.

Politics and Economic Policy in the Pre-Reform Period

On the eve of reform, China was governed by a fragmented leadership still recovering from the political turmoil of the Cultural Revolution. To some, Mao's death in September 1976 and the downfall of the Gang of Four a month later signaled the end of the revolutionary excesses of the previous decade, during which Maoists purged vast numbers of the Communist Party elite. Chief among those was Deng, who would later play a central role in reform. On returning to power, Deng's faction sought to challenge the weak authority of Hua Guofeng, Mao's handpicked successor, who sought to wrap himself in the mantle of Mao's authority and legacy by promulgating a policy of "two whatevers."[2] Hua's efforts to sideline Deng proved ineffective. Although Hua held powerful official titles, Deng had the backing of a strong political base consisting of senior party officials and veteran bureaucrats, the People's

---

[2] Joseph Fewsmith, *Dilemmas of Reform in China: Political Conflict and Economic Debate*, Armonk, N.Y.: M. E. Sharpe, 1994, p. 20. The "two whatevers" refers to the statement that "we will resolutely uphold whatever policy decisions Chairman Mao made, and unswervingly follow whatever instructions Chairman Mao gave" that first appeared in a February 1977 editorial. See Yan Sun, *The Chinese Reassessment of Socialism, 1976–1992*, Princeton, N.J.: Princeton University Press, 1995, pp. 23–24.

Liberation Army, and the intelligentsia (many of whom suffered greatly under the Maoists).[3]

On the economic side, the death of Mao and the subsequent end of the Cultural Revolution allowed China's leaders the opportunity to address chronic issues that had emerged during that revolution, such as stagnant growth of agriculture and living conditions and inefficiencies in the industrial sector. The government under Hua attempted to rehabilitate the command economic system by rebuilding the administrative institutions that had atrophied during the Cultural Revolution while simultaneously planning for a dramatic acceleration of economic growth.[4] A grandiose program of development laid out in the Ten-Year Plan of Economic Development 1976–1985 emphasized investments in heavy industry, particularly the import of complete plants from industrialized nations.[5] In the countryside, Hua touted the Dazhai model of collectivized agriculture and promoted the rapid mechanization of the rural sector.[6] Economic policy prior to the reform period attempted to replicate the massive industrialization and collectivization of agriculture inspired by the Soviet Union and implemented by China prior to the Cultural Revolution.

The ambitious goals laid out in the Ten-Year Plan quickly proved impossible to achieve. Faulty planning overestimated the capabilities of the economy, resulting in an unsustainable commitment of resources

---

3 Maurice Meisner, *The Deng Xiaoping Era: An Inquiry into the Fate of Chinese Socialism, 1978–1994*, New York: Hill and Wang, 1996, pp. 88–89. Deng's case for leadership was helped by a disastrous oil rig explosion in the Bohai Gulf and the roughly simultaneous drop in production at the Daqing oil field, both of which further damaged the political standing of Hua and his supporters. The poor performance of the People's Liberation Army in Vietnam also enabled Deng to sideline military leaders who were aligned with Hua.

4 Barry Naughton, *Growing Out of the Plan: Chinese Economic Reform 1978–1993*, New York: Cambridge University Press, 1996, pp. pp. 64–65.

5 Naughton, 1996, pp. 68–69.

6 The Dazhai model, named for the poor and barren region of Shanxi Province in which it came into being, took "the production brigade as the basic unit of account, [abolished] the cultivation of private plots, and [emphasized] ideological rather than material incentives" (Fewsmith, 1994, p. 20).

to an unrealistic wish list of projects.[7] Meanwhile, calls for the rapid mechanization of the rural sector failed to account for the inability of impoverished rural communes to purchase agricultural machinery, leaving in place the bottleneck of stagnant agricultural production.[8] The final nail in the coffin was the collapse of China's petroleum production in the late 1970s. China's economic planners had envisioned using hard currency earned from petroleum exports to fund foreign technology imports.[9] The complete failure to locate new oil-producing fields in 1978 after years of promising returns, coupled with the peaking of output in existing fields, dashed those designs,[10] and China's leaders realized the country's development required a different approach.

With economic performance lagging, Hua's political position became increasingly precarious. To counter Hua's "two whatevers," Deng and his allies extolled the principles of "seeking truth from facts" and making "practice the sole criterion of truth."[11] The "practice faction," as they came to be known, sought to repudiate the ultraleftists' radical policies and ideology and quickly garnered the support of veteran party officials purged during the Cultural Revolution. At the Third Plenum in December 1978, several Deng allies, notably the veteran economic planner Chen Yun and Deng's protégé Hu Yaobang, were elevated to high-level positions in the Party hierarchy, thus assuring Deng's ascendance.[12] Over the next two years, the remaining "whateverists" gradually fell from power, opening the door to the economic reform of the next decade.

China's Experience with Opening up and Reform

China's debates over economic policy saw officials fall into the two broad camps of reformers and conservatives. Deng—along with his

---

7 Naughton, 1996, pp. 70–71.

8 Fewsmith, 1994, p. 20.

9 Naughton,1996, p. 71.

10 Naughton, 1996, pp. 71–74.

11 Sun, 1995, pp. 24–31.

12 Meisner, 1996, p. 98.

proteges Hu (Party General Secretary) and Zhao (Premier)—formed the core of the former; Chen (Chair of the Central Advisory Commission)—along with fellow conservatives Li Xiannian (President), Yao Yilin (Vice-Premier), and, after 1987, Li Peng (Premier)—formed the core of the latter grouping. Generally speaking, the reformers favored faster economic growth and deeper integration into the world economy; they were comfortable with more-extensive use of market signals and material incentives; and they were willing to tolerate higher trade imbalances and levels of inflation than conservatives saw as acceptable. Conservatives prioritized steady, measured growth; they emphasized the necessity of central control over the economy and the leading roles of the state and the plan; and they viewed integration into the world economy with trepidation. The dividing line between the groups was not always clear. For example, the degree of support that Deng extended to market reforms and opening up generally depended on two factors: the extent to which reforms incurred political opposition from conservatives, and the extent to which economic reforms could be carried out without also undertaking political reforms.

The remaking of the Chinese economy during the first decade of the reforms can be divided into two broad waves. The period from 1979 to the end of 1980 marked the first wave, which saw the beginnings of agricultural liberalization and enterprise reform. Backlash over perceived departures from ideology and concerns over an overheating economy saw the conservatives assert control over economic policy in December 1980. As positive developments in the economy undercut conservative concerns, the second phase of reform began in 1984 and ended in 1988, when rapid inflation attendant on price decontrols led to protests that hardliners (such as Li and Yao) used to persuade Deng to shift control of managing the economy away from Zhao. The Tiananmen Square tragedy and Zhao's ensuing ouster saw conservatives dominate economic decisionmaking until 1992, when the failure of hardline economic policies led Deng to reassert the need for reforms leading to greater use of market signals and spurring the economic takeoff that has largely persisted to the present day.

Developments in Rural Reform

Economic reform saw early success in the rural sector, where collectivized farming gradually gave way to the liberalization of agriculture. In 1978, peasants in Anhui Province—with the tacit support of local cadres—adopted a "household responsibility system" that shifted production responsibility from the collective to the household, permitting families to retain (and even sell) any over-quota agricultural output, thereby incentivizing farmers to work hard and capture the gains of their labor.[13] Although successful, the experiments drew strong condemnation from those opposed to changes in the socialist system of ownership; such opposition resulted in these experiments being confined initially to poor and mountainous regions.[14] Opposition was particularly strong in wealthy coastal provinces that had a relatively successful track record of developing collective economies.[15] However, by 1982, the household responsibility system had spread to more than 72 percent of production teams in China.[16]

Several factors contributed to widespread proliferation of the system. First, the resulting high yields in agricultural productivity undercut efforts by conservatives to roll back the household responsibility system.[17] Second, the household responsibility system possessed strong political backing, first by provincial officials (such as Wan) and later on by national leaders (such as Deng); this backing was informed by data gathered by local party officials and extrabureaucratic organizations (such as the Rural Development Research Group).[18] Third,

---

13 Peasants contracted land, other resources, and output quotas to individual households. See Fewsmith, 1994, pp. 27–28; also see Kate Xiao Zhou, *How the Farmers Changed China: Power of the People*, New York: WestView Press, 1996.

14 Fewsmith, 1994, pp. 30–31. Areas where the household responsibility system first took off, or spread fastest, were often those that had suffered most during the famine and were at risk of renewed food shortage. Political leaders from these regions included future Premier and later Party General Secretary Zhao and future Vice-Premier Wan Li.

15 Fewsmith, 1994, p. 44.

16 Fewsmith, 1994, p. 48.

17 Fewsmith, 1994, pp. 48–49.

18 Fewsmith, 1994, pp 48–49.

the countryside proved too vast for the central bureaucracy to exert control over, thus giving local officials more breathing room to pursue reform.[19]

Although the early returns of rural reforms were a resounding success, peasants eventually encountered bureaucratic barriers. These included difficulty selling crops and inability to move goods from one area to the other.[20] Reforms implemented in 1983 attempted to address these issues by permitting the further loosening of the agricultural sector and the tacit acceptance of hired labor.[21] The latter was a contentious issue; conservatives equated hired labor with the restoration of capitalism in the countryside.[22] However, the continued growth in rural incomes and living standards provided political capital to Deng and other economic liberalizers, thus enabling the reforms to proceed.

Not all reforms in the agricultural sector met with success. Under political pressure in 1985 to address overproduction, the heavy burden of grain subsidies, and the need to direct funds into comprehensive urban reform, then-Premier Zhao attempted to abolish the state's monopoly on grain procurement and sales and replace it with a contract-based system.[23] However, the policy failed to address disparities between the set prices of the contracts with the state and the fluctuating prices of grain on the market, thus disincentivizing peasant willingness to engage in the contracts.[24] The result was a precarious decline in grain production that elicited conservative criticism and halted major agricultural reforms for the duration of Zhao's remaining years in power.

---

[19] Fewsmith, 1994, pp 48–49.

[20] Fewsmith, 1994, p. 124.

[21] Fewsmith, 1994, p. 124

[22] Fewsmith, 1994, p. 124.

[23] Under this system, peasants entered into voluntary contracts with the state to sell an agreed on amount of grain for a set price, allowing peasants to sell the surplus on the free market. Fewsmith, 1994, p. 154.

[24] Fewsmith, 1994, p. 156.

Developments in Enterprise Reform

Enterprise reform proceeded at a much slower pace than agricultural reform. This was because of the outsized role of the state in industry, the greater connections between industry and national power, and the regime's perceptions that its own survival prospects were tied to its control over urban areas because of their importance to the country's political life. Control over urban areas was viewed as much more important than control of the rural portions of the country. The relative laxity of state control in the countryside allowed reforms to emerge locally with the tacit acceptance of party officials; industry was wholly integrated into the state apparatus, with vested bureaucratic interests that blunted the pace of reform.[25] Reforms in the enterprise sector therefore proceeded in what Naughton describes as a classic *fang-shou* (放-受) policy cycle, with periods of energetic reforms (or "letting go" [*fang*]) followed by retrenchment (or "recovery" of state control [*shou*]).[26]

The economic policymakers who led enterprise reform did not endorse wholesale economic transformation. Rather, they advocated reforms to the status quo through the piecemeal introduction of market concepts into the plan. Economists in the late 1970s attempted to rehabilitate "objective economic laws," such as the law of value, to provide a Marxian rationale for economic reform.[27] Although a minority of economists supported radical market reforms, the main line of economic thinking sought an "organic integration" of plan and market that would see market forces play a role in achieving a socialist end.[28]

Early experiments in enterprise reform sought to adjust the relationship between enterprises and the state. According to proponents of this line of thinking, administrative constraints imposed by the state prevented enterprises from operating at their productive potential. This view was opposed by two camps in the 1970s—those who desired a stronger role for the state and those who sought to relegate administra-

---

25 Fewsmith, 1994, p. 56.

26 Naughton, 1996, p. 98.

27 Meisner, 1996, p. 211.

28 See Fewsmith, 1994, pp. 66–70; and Meisner, 1996, p. 213.

tive authority to the provinces.[29] In late 1978, Sichuan Province began trial experiments with expanded enterprise autonomy, the success of which led to the implementation of experimental enterprise autonomy nationwide in 1979.[30] Along with granting enterprise managers greater decisionmaking powers over production and marketing, reforms also included profit retention to incentivize productivity and the creation of five special economic zones (SEZs) (经济特区).[31]

Although the aforementioned measures introduced a modicum of efficiency and productivity in enterprises, substantial issues remained. Some degree of flexibility emerged at the basic level, but enterprises remained hindered by their links to the wider economic bureaucracy.[32] Furthermore, these reforms were carried out in an environment in which the price structure remained irrational: Little FDI existed; private property and intellectual property were largely unprotected by any meaningful legal structures; technological sophistication was low; quality control was virtually nonexistent; and provincial authorities routinely discriminated against or even banned goods made in other provinces.[33] The resulting economic problems gave conservatives ammunition to criticize a reform program that they perceived as too radical a departure from their economic and ideological beliefs. By late 1980, the reform program ground to a halt.

The period between 1980 and 1982 saw a retrenchment of reform, with conservatives led by Chen imposing tighter economic and ideological controls. Their apprehension toward earlier reforms belied a belief in the primacy of a planned economy in which market forces merely played a supplementary role.[34] Proper planning, conservatives argued, must be maintained to prevent macroeconomic imbalances

---

[29] Fewsmith, 1994, p. 73.

[30] Naughton, 1996, pp. 99–100.

[31] Naughton, 1996, p. 101.

[32] Naughton, 1996, p. 119.

[33] Fewsmith, 1994, p. 115.

[34] For an expanded discussion of the views of Chen Yun and his followers, see Fewsmith, 1994, pp. 88–89.

and economic disorder. By the end of 1982, however, conservative predictions of economic difficulty and slow growth were swept aside by positive developments in the economic situation.[35] With their warnings undermined, the reform agenda returned to the forefront of Chinese economic policy.

The second wave of industrial reform (between 1984 and 1988) began under a set of circumstances different from the first. Improved economic conditions, the experiences of the first reform period, and Deng's enhanced authority all contributed to a reform program that was stronger and wider in scope. Furthermore, this period saw noted reformer Zhao emerge as a central figure in the reform process, having carved out enough political leverage to emerge from Chen's shadow as the primary driver of economic policy.[36]

The reform program introduced in 1984 contained elements of earlier reforms. Enterprise autonomy was expanded with such reforms as a factory manager responsibility system, long-term profit contracting, the linking of wages to profit, and output autonomy.[37] These reforms sought to improve incentives for enterprises to operate in a market. A second emerging development was the initiation of a dual-track system that greatly expanded the role of market forces in which a planned economy and a growing market economy coexisted. The system emerged as a compromise with conservatives who insisted on partitioning the economy into plan and market sectors.[38] However, by fixing the absolute size of the plan, reformists were able to marginalize the importance of the planned economy as the market economy expanded.[39]

Debates over economic policy in the late 1980s primarily centered on the rapid rate of growth and associated issues, such as inflation and continuing trade imbalances. Conservatives expressed alarm at imbalances caused by high growth rates and argued for the imposition

---

35 Fewsmith, 1994, pp. 128–129.

36 Naughton, 1996, p. 178.

37 Naughton, 1996, p. 205.

38 Naughton, 1996, p. 182.

39 Naughton, 1996, p. 220.

of greater central controls.[40] Reformists fell into two camps: The first was characterized by economists such as Wu Jinglian, who supported a tight monetary policy and radical price reform;[41] the latter, as represented by economists of the Economic Reform Institute, emphasized microeconomic changes, particularly ownership reform.[42]

Deng's demand that Zhao press ahead with price decontrols at the end of 1987 and Zhao's failure to rein in the consequent inflation from such decontrols in 1988 resulted in the return of conservatives to the forefront of economic policymaking and helped spur the student and broader public protests that exploded in April–June 1989. The aftermath of the regime's decision to crush these protests at Tiananmen Square in 1989 solidified the positions of such hardliners as Li and Yao, who worked together to institute a conservative economic program centered on macroeconomic austerity, recentralization, and preferential treatment for state-owned industries.[43] However, the conservatives' dominance was short-lived as efforts to cool down the economy and reduce inflation pushed the economy into a recession and opened the door for Deng's final push to transform China into a more market-driven economy from 1992 onward.

Similarities and Differences Between China Then and North Korea Now

China in the 1970s and North Korea today are nominally Marxist-Leninist states under one-party rule, but there is a stark contrast in the exercise of power. Kim appears to have consolidated his position as the absolute ruler of North Korea, especially in aftermath of several high-profile purges.[44] By contrast, although Deng held immense political power following the 1978 Third Plenum, his standing was that of

---

40 Fewsmith, 1994, pp. 150–151.

41 Fewsmith, 1994, p. 198.

42 Fewsmith, 1994, p. 198.

43 Naughton, 1996, p. 274.

44 A notable example is the purge of his powerful uncle, Jang Song-Thaek, in 2013. See Alexandre Mansourov, "North Korea: The Dramatic Fall of Jang Song Thaek," *38 North*, December 9, 2013.

a first among equals, as evidenced by his rivalry with Chen, who led the conservative opposition to market reforms throughout the 1980s.[45] This difference, perhaps more than any other in this analysis, stands out as important: Deng could be criticized indirectly (and his key lieutenants attacked directly); Kim does not appear to be subject to similar constraints on his authority.

Domestically, both China and North Korea have suffered terrible famines. But in the case of China, the death of the regime's key founder (Mao) opened the way for some successors who did not tie themselves to his legacy, with Deng leading an effort to reach a verdict on Mao that found him to have been 70 percent correct and 30 percent in error. This, again, differs substantially from North Korea's situation: Kim's authority stems from his status as the inheritor of the "bloodline of Mangyongdae," with his grandfather Kim Il-Sung and his father Kim Jong-Il given the titles of "eternal leaders of Juche Korea" in the revised 2016 Constitution.

On the international stage, the situation that China faced in the late 1970s differs somewhat from the one that North Korea faces today. By 1978, China and the United States were well on their way to normalization of ties; Beijing had claimed a permanent seat on the United Nations Security Council, and the rival regime in Taipei looked increasingly isolated. Relations with the Soviet Union, although not as tense as they had been at the high point of Sino-Soviet conflict in the late 1960s, were still fraught, given Moscow's invasion of Afghanistan, its stationing of large numbers of armored divisions on the border between the two nations, and its support for the Vietnamese invasion of Cambodia; all of these factors served to drive Beijing and Washington closer.[46]

North Korea faces no external threat driving it toward the United States; rather, Pyongyang sees an existential threat in the United States and its allies. Additionally, China's size and sense of confidence from having fought the United States in Korea in the 1950s and in Viet-

---

[45] Fewsmith, 1994, p. 8.

[46] For a discussion of Sino-Soviet threat perceptions in the late 1970s, see Jonathan D. Pollack, *The Sino-Soviet Rivalry and Chinese Security Debate*, Santa Monica, Calif.: RAND Corporation, R-2907-AF, 1982, pp. 37–38.

nam in the 1960s and 1970s differs completely from North Korea's experience of having been defeated and nearly destroyed by the United States in 1950 and stymied in its efforts to overturn that defeat in the decades since. At the same time, some of North Korea's military capabilities in 2019 compare favorably with China's military capabilities circa 1978, even though its territory and population size provide it with no prospect of trading blows or giving up space for time the way China planned to in the event of war with the United States.

In some important ways in the economic sphere, North Korea shares similar traits with China at the onset of reform. Both possess(ed) factor endowments conducive toward economic growth, such as poor use of rural-based human capital and low wages, age structures favorable to growth, and proximity to large, advanced markets.[47] For the last factor in particular, shared cultural links with immediate neighbors provide added impetus—China's experience with advanced economies, such as Hong Kong and Taiwan, and the potential for cooperation between North Korea and South Korea.[48] In terms of economic challenges, both countries lack(ed) market mechanisms and institutions, although black markets are probably more advanced in North Korea today than they were in China in 1978.[49] North Korea's nascent private sector was birthed in the aftermath of the 1994–1998 famine and, although technically still illegal, now accounts for as much as 30 percent to 50 percent of DPRK gross domestic product (GDP).[50]

---

[47] Naughton, 1994, pp. 51–54.

[48] For example, see Naubahar Sharif and Mitchell M. Tseng, "The Role of Hong Kong in Mainland China's Modernization in Manufacturing," *Asian Survey*, Vol. 51, No. 4, July/August 2011. For a case study of Fujian Province's experience with Taiwan, see Keun Lee, Byung-Yeon Kim, and Insook Lee, "The Possibility of Economic Reform in North Korea," *Journal of Contemporary Asia*, Vol. 39, No. 2, May 2009. According to one former Republic of Korea (ROK) government official, trade and FDI integration with South Korea could boost DPRK annual GDP growth rates by 3 percent. See Jong-Wha Lee and Ju Hyun Pyun, "North Korea's Economic Integration and Growth Potential," *Asian Economic Journal*, Vol. 32, No. 3, September 2018.

[49] Although some petty entrepreneurship existed, on the whole, the state maintained a tight monopoly on commercial activities. See Naughton, 1996, pp. 45–46.

[50] Andrei Lankov, *The Resurgence of a Market Economy in North Korea*, Moscow: Carnegie Moscow Center, 2016, p. 1.

In terms of foreign trade, both countries experienced low exposure to the wider world. In 1978, China's total trade accounted for less than 1 percent of the world's total.[51] North Korea has similarly low levels of foreign trade, the majority of which is conducted with China. Since 2014, total trade has declined precipitously for multiple reasons; sanctions and the closure of the Kaesong Industrial Complex are two of the most important factors.[52] The sanctions regime imposed on North Korea provides an additional impediment to expanding international trade, one that China did not face at the onset of opening and reform. Additionally, China's emergence on the international trade and investment scene occurred at a time when a country could plausibly employ a strategy of moving low-cost, unproductive labor out of the countryside and into factories to produce low-quality goods for export; if North Korea sought to replicate this pathway today, it would be hampered by substantially greater competition from other nations, the growth of automation, on-demand 3D printing, and already highly entrenched international production chains.

Finally, at the time of China's opening and reform, no communist party had ever fallen from power because of internal collapse (though two—Hungary and Czechoslovakia—had been toppled by Soviet intervention intended to head off such a possibility). China's leaders watched the growth of the Solidarity movement in Poland and Charter 77 in Czechoslovakia with concern,[53] and they saw the Soviet Union's simultaneous pursuit of economic and political restructuring (through Mikhail Gorbachev's policies of glasnost and perestroika) as overly risky, but even they did not foresee the ultimate collapse of Eastern European communism and the dissolution of the Soviet empire. By contrast, the Korean Workers Party and the Kim family regime are well aware of the risks of

---

51 Information Office of the State Council, *China's Foreign Trade*, Beijing, December 2011.

52 "Total Trade," North Korea in the World, webpage, undated.

53 Solidarity was a Polish nongovernmental trade union begun in 1980 by Lech Walesa and others that became a broad anti-bureaucratic social movement, using methods of civil resistance to advance the causes of workers' rights and social change. Charter 77 was a civic initiative in the Czechoslovak Socialist Republic from 1976 to 1992, named after the document Charter 77, which criticized the government for failing to implement human rights provisions of a number of documents it had signed.

regime collapse that might result from reforming the economic system or, even more so, the political system. As a result, DPRK uses equivalents of China's SEZs to prevent the spread of information, values, and economic incentives outside state control, thereby reducing the possibility of a wider societal call for openness that might get out of control. North Korea under Kim Jong-Un has a lower degree of willingness to run risks than China held in the late 1970s. This makes sense: China was striving to compete with other great powers and other leading Asian economies; in contrast, the DPRK regime's goals appear substantially more limited to survival and, if possible, the reversal of the defeat it suffered in the Korean War. This is a key contextual distinction between the Chinese and DPRK experiences in this domain.

Factors That Influenced Vietnam's Economic Reform Decisions

What were the drivers of economic reform in Vietnam? Does the pathway that Vietnam went down in deciding on and carrying out economic reform provide any insights that might be useful for assessing the motives, possible pitfalls, and trajectory that North Korea might follow if it decides to open up its economy? In this section, we explore similarities and differences between the two countries before turning to a brief examination of Vietnam's experience and concluding with an analysis of what the Vietnam case means for North Korea.

Vietnam and North Korea share some similarities as communist nations, notably their shared Marxist-Leninist ideology and aspects of the party-state-military political structure, but not much beyond that. In North Korea, Kim rules as a living god over a totalitarian regime; the VCP runs Vietnam through a collective leadership comprising the "four pillar" (*tu tru*) institutions run by the VCP general secretary (Nguyen Phu Trong), the prime minister (Nguyen Xuan Phuc), the president (also Trong), and the chairman of the national assembly (Nguyen Thi Kim Nagan).[54] This fragmented system of authority means that decisions often emerge only after months or even years of painstaking negotiation.[55] With Kim the primary or sole decisionmaker, he can probably formulate and implement policy decisions very quickly; thus, the DPRK leadership can move much more quickly than Vietnam's leadership when it chooses to do so.

The countries also have key differences in their economic systems. Vietnam loosened strict adherence to a planned economy in favor of market Leninism in the late 1980s under its *doi moi* policy; North Korea has mostly resisted external market forces. The VCP's decision to engage in *doi moi* was primarily the result of socialist state institutions failing to improve people's livelihoods.[56] Hanoi began its economic reforms while under international economic sanctions for its invasion of Cambodia in 1978; it was forced to accelerate these efforts by the collapse of its Soviet patrons in 1991.[57] *Doi moi* authorized a return to private initiative in the economy, encouraged foreign

---

54 President Tran Dai Quang's death in September 2018 has caused some consolidation of these four separate positions. General Secretary Nguyen Phu Trong has since assumed the presidency as well. This is exceptionally rare in Vietnamese politics—the most recent example preceding this was in 1986, when General Secretary Truong Chinh briefly held both positions. Ho Chi Minh, the founder of communist Vietnam, held both titles from 1951 until his death in 1969. But as a general rule, consolidation of positions is considered unusual and has prompted some concerned analysis that Truong is poised to become the next "strongman" of Vietnam or "Xi Jinping of Vietnam." See Paul Schuler and Mai Truong, "Leadership Reshuffle and the Future of Vietnam's Collective Leadership," *Perspective*, Vol. 2019, No. 9, ISEAS Yusof Ishak Institute, February 22, 2019.

55 Party congresses became routinized in 1975. Prior to that, they were held less often and less predictably.

56 For example, see Melanie Beresford, *National Unification and Economic Development in Vietnam*, Basingstoke, UK: MacMillan, 1989a; Melanie Beresford, "Vietnam Socialist Agriculture in Transition," *Journal of Contemporary Asia*, Vol. 24, No. 4, 1989b, Adam Fforde, "Review of *Profit and Poverty in Rural Vietnam: Winners and Losers of a Dismantled Revolution*" (by Rita Liljestrom, Eva Lindskog, Nguyen Van Anh, and Vuong Xuan Tinh), *Journal of Asian Studies*, Vol. 58, No. 3, 1999; and Adam Fforde and Stefan deVylder, *From Plan to Market: The Economic Transition in Vietnam*, Boulder, Colo.: Westview Press, 1996.

57 For an authoritative overview of this history, see Carlyle A. Thayer, "Vietnam's Foreign Policy in an Era of Rising Sino-U.S. Competition and Increasing Domestic Political Influence," *Asian Security*, Vol. 13, No. 3, July 31, 2017.

trade and direct investment, and stabilized price levels and exchange rates.[58] These changes, according to the 2019 World Bank overview of Vietnam, "have spurred rapid economic growth and development and transformed Vietnam from one of the world's poorest nations to a lower middle-income country."[59] Vietnam's GDP, now approximately $241 billion, has increased thirtyfold in the past three decades, and its total trade stands at approximately $425 billion.[60] Vietnam has been called an "Asian tiger" and is now ranked 47th in GDP and 35th in purchasing power parity worldwide. These are impressive accomplishments, considering that the country in 1988 had approximately 3 million people suffering from starvation and 5 million malnourished within its borders.[61]

As part of *doi moi*, Hanoi sought normalization of economic and broader overall relations with China, ending years of tension following the countries' 1979 war. The VCP also authorized economic interactions with other countries as a way to reduce Vietnam's economic dependence on China and to otherwise support Vietnamese national interests.[62] In May 1988, VCP leaders announced Resolution Number 13, which stressed the need for Vietnam to make "more friends, fewer enemies" by forging a multidirectional foreign policy.[63] This led to

---

58 David Dollar, "The Hanoi Summit Shines a Light on the 'Vietnam Model' of Development," Brookings Institution, February 27, 2019.

59 World Bank, "The World Bank in Vietnam: Overview," October 15, 2018.

60 For analysis of Vietnam's economic progress over the past 30 years, see Le Hong Hiep, "The Vietnam Model for North Korea," *Project Syndicate*, February 26, 2019.

61 Huong Le Thu, "Can Vietnam's Doi Moi Reforms Be an Inspiration for North Korea?" ASAN Forum, August 23, 2018.

62 Le Hong Hiep, *Living Next to the Giant: The Political Economy of Vietnam's Relations with China Under Doi Moi*, Institute of Southeast Asian Studies (ISEAS)–Yusof Ishak Institute, 2017; Le Hong Hiep, "Vietnam's Domestic-Foreign Policy Nexus: *Doi Moi*, Foreign Policy Reform, and Sino-Vietnamese Normalization," *Asian Politics & Policy*, Vol. 5, No. 3, June 25, 2013.

63 Resolution Number 13, along with many other VCP resolutions, remain classified within Vietnam. In this case, our quotations of Resolution Number 13 were cited in Tung Nguyen Vu, "Chapter 8: Vietnam's Security Challenges: Hanoi's New Approach to National Security and Implications to Defense and Foreign Policies," in National Institute for Defense Stud-

an emphasis on pursuing relations with the Association for Southeast Asian Nations, Japan, and Europe, and on a "step by step" basis with the United States.[64]

Drivers of *Doi Moi*

Following North Vietnam's conquest of South Vietnam in 1975, the country was renamed the Socialist Republic of Vietnam (SRV); just ten years later, the SRV was on the brink of total socioeconomic collapse, prompting the VCP to radically reconsider the wisdom of maintaining strict adherence to a planned economy. At the Sixth Party Congress in 1986, the VCP decided to forge ahead with *doi moi*. VCP leaders determined that one-party rule could remain intact while farmers, industrialists, and entrepreneurs were permitted to conduct their business with less interference from the state.

At least six main drivers pushed the VCP toward *doi moi*. We explore these here. First, prior to 1986, the VCP had mandated that farmers and industrialists rely on the state for their supplies. However, the SRV was perpetually behind the curve in delivering supplies in a timely and efficient manner.[65] People were also regularly affected by command economy inefficiencies. Particularly in the run up to *doi moi*, from 1975 to 1985, supplies of consumer goods were woefully

---

ies, *Asia Pacific Countries' Security Outlook and its Implications for the Defense Sector*, Tokyo, NIDS Joint Research Series No. 5, 2010.

64 See Thayer, 2017; Carlyle A. Thayer, "Vietnam's Foreign Policy in an Era of Rising Sino-U.S. Competition: Providing Equity to the Major Powers While Pursuing Proactive International Integration," presentation to Conference on Great Power Rivalries, Domestic Politics, and Southeast Asian Foreign Policy, The Dorothy Borg Research Project, Weatherhead East Asia Institute, Columbia University, November 10–11, 2016; Hiep, 2013; Phan Doan Nam, "Ngoai giao Viet Nam sau 20 nam doi moi [Vietnam's Diplomacy After 20 Years]," *Tap Chi Cong San [Communist Review]*, July 14, 2006; Nguyen Manh Hung, "Thuc hien nhat quan dong loi doi ngoai doc lap, tu chu, hoa binh, hop tac va phat trien [Consistently Implementing the Foreign Policy of Independence, Autonomy, Peace, and Development]," *Tap Chi Cong San [Communist Review]*, September 17, 2006. According to Hiep, many VCP resolutions have been referenced or excerpted in *Tap Chi Cong San [Communist Review]* by Vietnamese researchers associated with government-affiliated think tanks; we cite those in this report.

65 Jonathan London, "Viet Nam and the Making of Market-Leninism," *Pacific Review*, Vol. 22, No. 3, July 2009.

inadequate.[66] Food scarcity had become a severe problem in the 1970s before the supply rebounded by the early 1980s.[67] Consumer goods were the product of industry, but industrialization could not fully occur without first releasing the labor on farms, which meant raising the scale of agricultural production through mechanization and technological improvement.[68] Ultimately, Hanoi became locked into the worst of both worlds: It was unable to produce desperately needed consumer goods and unable to raise enough food to provide for its people. Adding to the misery, a currency crisis, which saw hyperinflation rise to 775 percent in 1985, elevated the sense of urgency to fix the economy.[69] Other socioeconomic problems also plagued Vietnam: unemployment (or underemployment), housing shortages, and limited government services in education and health care. To take unemployment as an example, the period from 1981 to 1985 witnessed only 15 percent of first-time work-eligible Vietnamese able to find employment—out of a population of 7 million youths.[70] These factors yielded an economy with 70 percent of the labor force working in agriculture, making Vietnam one of the poorest countries in Asia at the time.[71]

Second, because the state was so inept at providing basic goods for production, state-owned enterprise (SOE) employees were incentivized toward black market trading, which led to widespread corrup-

---

66 If we take production goals in 1980 as an example, food only reached 69 percent of its target. Other missed production goals were coal at 52 percent, electricity at 72 percent, sea fisheries at 40 percent, cotton fabrics at 39 percent, and paper at 37 percent. For more, see Vu Tuan Anh, ed., *Vietnam's Economic Reform: Results and Problems*, Hanoi: Social Science Publishing House, 1994.

67 Quan Hoang Vuong, Dam Van Nhue, Daniel van Houtte, and Tri Dung Tran, "The Entrepreneurial Facets as Precursor to Vietnam's Economic Renovation in 1986," *IUP Journal of Entrepreneurship Development*, Vol. VIII, No. 4, 2011.

68 William J. Duiker, "Ideology and Nation-Building in the Democratic Republic of Vietnam," *Asian Survey*, Vol. 17, No. 5, 1977.

69 Quan Hoang Vuong, "Vietnam's Political Economy in Transition (1986–2016)," *Stratfor*, May 27, 2014.

70 Quan Hoang Vuong et al., 2011.

71 Bui Tat Thang, "After the War: 25 Years of Economic Development in Vietnam," (commentary), *NIRA Review*, Tokyo: National Institute for Research Advancement, Spring 2000.

tion.[72] Corruption itself was not new for Vietnam, but corruption at this precarious moment in SRV history significantly contributed to the further decline of SOE productivity. Those running illegal businesses continued receiving state subsidies while shirking became prevalent, thus further depressing productivity.[73]

Third, the VCP's conquest of South Vietnam brought difficulties even as the regime sought to use it to lay claims to nationalist legitimacy. The South Vietnamese were accustomed to capitalism, and anger and resistance were a consequence of VCP efforts to integrate South Vietnam's open economy into North Vietnam's centrally planned communist system.[74] For one thing, forced collectivization diminished or eliminated past profits in agriculture. In addition, the Party viewed as "suspect" people with certain class backgrounds, most notably ex–South Vietnamese leaders and the wealthy, who were subject to exclusion unless put through political "rehabilitation."[75]

Fourth, the death of Party legend Le Duan was another key factor in prompting the VCP to enact *doi moi* reforms. An original member of the communist revolutionary movement and cofounder of the Indochina Communist Party in 1930, he was a trusted adviser to the father of communist Vietnam, Ho Chi Minh, and Ho selected him to become First Party Secretary in 1959. Le Duan became General Secretary in 1960 and remained in that position until his death in 1986. Prior to the Sixth Party Congress, he had been ill for many years and had struggled to read the Party's report at the Fifth Party Congress in 1982.[76] His death was important because it offered an opportunity to shift the VCP away from incremental changes to the command economy—Le Duan had actually supported many reforms—toward a bolder and wholesale reimagination of Vietnam's economic model.

---

72 London, 2009.

73 London, 2009.

74 Duiker, 1977.

75 Duiker, 1977; London, 2009.

76 Nguyen Van Canh, *Vietnam Under Communism, 1975–1982*, Stanford, Calif.: Stanford University, Hoover Institution Press, 2017.

Fresh leaders would also have the opportunity to express their views and finally be in the position of decisionmaking.[77] One of them in particular, Nguyen Van Linh, who served as general secretary from 1986 to 1991, was instrumental in pushing *doi moi* forward. Linh had served as party secretary of Ho Chi Minh City since 1975 and was an advocate of market-based reforms. He was given fairly wide latitude to deviate from Party ideology (even though he was briefly removed from the Politburo), probably because of his experience as a communist revolutionary and for having served as a leading political figure for the Viet Cong during the war.

Fifth, Vietnam's 1978 invasion of Cambodia put a severe drain on already depleted state coffers, and the war resulted in Vietnam's further international isolation. The Association for Southeast Asian Nations—in conjunction with China, the United States, and other Western states—imposed economic sanctions on the SRV, with many parties canceling economic assistance altogether.[78] Soviet subsidies were insufficient to cover the shortfall in revenues. Of all countries involved, China was particularly incensed that Vietnam would attack its Khmer Rouge ally in Cambodia. Beijing subsequently launched attacks along the China-Vietnam land border in 1979 to "teach Vietnam a lesson," thus forcing Hanoi to expend even more resources. By 1982, Sino-Soviet relations had recovered sufficiently that Beijing was no longer as concerned about losing influence to the Soviets and their proxies in Indochina. China therefore sought to "bleed Vietnam white" by encouraging it to stay longer to fight insurgency in Cambodia.[79]

Finally, the series of economic reforms taking place within the Soviet Union in the mid-1980s had a significant impact on the

---

[77] One notable exception is the 1986 case of General Secretary Truong Chinh—a communist revolutionary who also strongly believed in the need for economic reforms and actively contributed to *doi moi*. Truong is given significant credit in Vietnam for the country's turn to market-Leninism.

[78] Vu Tuan Anh, 1994.

[79] Vu Tuan Anh, 1994.

VCP's decision to move forward with *doi moi*.[80] Perestroika, championed by Soviet leader Gorbachev, advocated transitioning SOEs into self-financing companies. Although potentially a form of revisionism according to Marxist ideologues, the SRV was able to accept the change to market economics, probably because it was coming from the originator of Hanoi's own state-run socialism and its primary benefactor. On the latter point, and for practical purposes, the VCP was compelled to respond to perestroika because it led the steady drying up of annual Soviet economic assistance to Vietnam; by 1990, aid had completely been curtailed.[81]

What *Doi Moi* Tells Us About Reform Prospects in North Korea

The period between North Vietnam's conquest of South Vietnam in 1975 and the Sixth Party Congress in 1986 featured a series of events that incentivized the VCP to undertake serious and systemic reforms to the command economy. Although North Korea probably shares the same trouble in delivering supplies to SOEs and goods and services to the people, it also would not seem to share any of the other indicators of reform. For example, the Kim regime has not conquered South Korea and therefore does not have to deal with the sticky questions of how best to expand its administrative grid on the Korean Peninsula to capitalist markets without sacrificing elements of control. In addition, Pyongyang probably controls SOEs to a much greater extent, given the reach of Kim's totalitarian regime compared with the "four centers" power model found in Vietnam. It is also questionable whether North Korea has any reformers in its ranks and, if it does, whether they are allowed to voice their unvarnished concerns and have real impact—put

---

80 The Soviet Union's perestroika had a significant impact on pushing the VCP toward *doi moi*, but it is very likely that leaders in Hanoi also closely assessed China's "reform and opening up" (*gaige kaifang*) in 1978. Masahiko Ebashi argues that China's reforms were one factor affecting Hanoi's thinking (Masahiko Ebashi, "The Economic Takeoff," in James W. Morley and Masashi Nishihara, eds., *Vietnam Joins the World*, New York: M. E. Sharpe, 1997, p. 40). The timing of *doi moi*'s announcement, however, coincided with a prolonged period of China-Vietnam hostility, suggesting that Chinese economic reform ideas might have been less impactful than perestroika.

81 Vu Tuan Anh, 1994.

another way, whether there are any Nguyen Van Linhs in North Korea. At present, it is hard to say, but Kim Il-Sung's death did not lead to any economic reforms of note; nor did Kim Jong-Il's death appear to have opened up much meaningful space for widespread and systematic reforms that could compare with *doi moi* in Vietnam. Finally, North Korea's economic reliance on China and Vietnam's dependence on the Soviet Union for assistance during the Cold War might be somewhat similar on the surface, but North Korea depends more on China than Vietnam did on the Soviet Union, and China today has far more resources than the Soviet Union had in the 1980s.

Factors That Influenced Cuban Economic Reform Decisions

The Cuban government of Fidel Castro came to power through a popular revolutionary uprising in 1959 that ousted U.S.-backed dictator Fulgencio Batista. The Castro regime consolidated power by adopting a communist model and allying with the Soviet Union. It survived the U.S.-sponsored 1961 Bay of Pigs invasion, the Central Intelligence Agency's Operation Mongoose plots to assassinate Castro, and a major U.S–Soviet standoff in 1962 over Russian attempts to emplace nuclear missiles on the island. This tumultuous early period crystallized what would become five decades of nearly unremitting U.S. hostility, including a comprehensive economic embargo designed to bring down the regime. Regime survival, characterized by two intertwined features—perpetuation of the personalistic dictatorship of Castro and the preservation of its state socialist model—was the overarching objective of the regime until 2006, when the ill and aging dictator relinquished power to his younger brother, Raúl Castro Ruz, who was formally elected president of the Council of State two years later. The younger Castro had served as chief of the army and de facto second in command for the preceding decades. Fidel Castro died in 2016, and Raúl Castro Ruz passed the reins to Miguel Diaz Canel in 2018, initiating Cuba's transition to the post-Castro era.

The dominant theme of political continuity in Cuba has been punctuated by two major periods in which the Cuban regime attempted, or was forced by circumstances, to open up to the world. Economic imperatives and emigration crises drove these fitful attempts at opening, though such measures were always carefully metered out of fear that political instability would ensue and the United States would capitalize on events to topple the regime. Fidel Castro deftly used both political repression and the fear of U.S. intervention to shore up his regime. He was the principal hardliner surrounded by various acolytes and apparatchiks of his revolutionary regime, who are only now passing from positions of power. His brother was known to be more pragmatic and to prefer the models of China and Vietnam of introducing market reforms while maintaining political controls. Various reformers occupied positions of power during the 1990s, somewhat tenuously, but the economic changes adopted in those years were designed to extract economic benefit without risking any loss of political control or delegitimizing the regime through increased inequalities that market socialism would inevitably bring.

The Barack Obama administration, having assessed that 60 years of sanctions and ostracism had not produced the desired reforms or regime change, decided to pursue an opening to Cuba. Raúl Castro Ruz responded positively through secret negotiations conducted by his son Alejandro with two White House officials. The official bureaucracies of both countries were kept in the dark because opponents of the opening likely would have squelched the effort. Although the subsequent restoration of formal diplomatic ties in July 2015 represented a historic milestone, the resulting economic and political changes in Cuba were relatively modest. U.S. legislation bars lifting the U.S. embargo until there are free elections and the Castro brothers have departed from power. To date, proposals to revise that legislation have not gained the necessary support.

For its part, Cuba appears far from a decision to hold free elections as of this writing. Fidel Castro's long-standing paranoia of U.S. intentions came to the fore on the heels of a historic visit by President Obama to Havana, where he was greeted by enthusiastic crowds eager to see the first U.S. African-American president. Castro and the official Cuban media denounced Obama's speech, and the 7th Party Congress, which convened shortly thereafter, refrained from any additional economic opening steps. Even Raúl Castro Ruz was compelled to issue assurances that Cuba would not become a multiparty democracy or adopt capitalism on his watch.

Cuba's modest economic reforms—self-employment for a half-million Cubans, foreign investment in tourism and other sectors, and generous subsidized oil supplies from Venezuela—have enabled it to limp along. However, the crisis in Venezuela, lack of any substantial new donors, and the periodic destruction from hurricanes augur continued hardship for the country. The advent of the Trump administration led to harsh rhetoric and revocation of some measures taken by the Obama administration to liberalize travel, remittance, and investment flows from the United States. For the time being, any Cuban propensity to open further appears to be checked by renewed official U.S. hostility and the continued U.S. economic embargo. Over the longer run, economic and sociopolitical changes in Cuba that were set in motion by the limited economic opening and increased travel and tourism—and by the passing of the revolutionary generation—will likely produce a slow transformation of Cuban society and its relationship with the world.

Factors in Cuban Decisionmaking

A Brief Warming in the 1970s

A brief opening by the Jimmy Carter administration led to the opening of a U.S. Interests Section in Havana and a Cuban Interests Section in Washington in 1977. Diplomatic efforts to create conditions for further opening did not bear fruit, and the Mariel exodus created significant concerns over instability in both Havana and Washington.[82] Periodic outflows were used by Castro to relieve pent-up pressure, but the outpourings also threatened political destabilization and possible retaliation from the United States.

[82] The Mariel exodus was a mass emigration of Cubans from Cuba's Mariel Harbor to the United States between April and October 1980.

Post-Soviet Shock and Reforms of the 1990s

The dissolution of the Soviet Union in 1991 precipitated a severe economic crisis and the specter of regime collapse in Cuba. Cuba had relied heavily on the Soviet Union and the Soviet bloc for imports, including vital oil supplies. In 1991, total imports from the Soviet Union shrank by 71 percent, and oil imports of 13 million metric tons in 1989 plummeted to 8.6 million metric tons just two years later.[83] The Council for Mutual Economic Assistance also dissolved as regime change swept the Soviet bloc; Cuba's total foreign trade dropped 75–80 percent between 1989 and 1991, and its GDP contracted by more than 30 percent.[84]

Under this excruciating economic pressure, the Cuban regime declared a variety of emergency measures in what it labeled "the Special Period in the Time of Peace." As food stocks dwindled, Cubans forced into near-starvation diets participated in an array of frenetic side hustles to make ends meet. The regime grudgingly legalized very limited entrepreneurial activity by Cubans and began to aggressively court foreign investment and state-sponsored joint ventures in tourism, nickel mining, medical services, and oil exploration. The national assembly passed the Constitutional Reform Law in 1992, authorizing the opening of farmer's markets, private markets for industrial and handmade products, and certain specified categories of self-employment.

Workers on state farms were allowed to form cooperatives to use the land; in 1993, Cubans were permitted to hold convertible current and foreign currencies as Cuba sought to stimulate tourism and other foreign investment. The convertible Cuban peso was introduced, foreign trade was decentralized, and duty-free zones and industrial parks were created through a series of decrees from 1994 to 1996. By 1997, 4,000 cooperatives had been created and 106,000 independent farms existed. By 1997, 160,000 self-employed Cubans, 162 foreign joint ventures, and 827 foreign private firms were operating. By the govern-

83 Edward Gonzalez and David Ronfeldt, *Cuba Adrift in a Postcommunist World*, Santa Monica, Calif.: RAND Corporation, R-4231-USDP, 1992, p. v.

84 Banco Central de Cuba, *Cuba's Banking and Financial System*, 2nd ed., 1998.

ment's assessment, government-owned state farms had shrunk from 74 percent to 24.4 percent of the total number of farms.[85]

The principal debates in the 1990s revolved around the pace and extent of economic reforms to be introduced, not a wholesale change in the one-party state. Cuba's Communist Party leadership agreed that the party should retain political power and the social safety net for Cubans. Fidel Castro was associated with the most-conservative positions; his brother was reputed to favor more-rapid adoption of market socialism along the lines of China and Vietnam.[86] Despite the economic crisis, Fidel Castro's hold on power was absolute, and no public or frontal challenge to him arose. The so-called *duros*, or hardliners, prevailed over the only publicly identified reformer when senior official and longtime Castro confident Carlos Aldana was dismissed from the Politburo and expelled from the party in October 1992 on corruption charges.

Raúl Castro Ruz was directly involved in promoting foreign investment through his position as the senior ranking general and minister of the Fuerzas Armadas Revolutionarias. The Cuban army was entrusted with leading investments in construction and with operating the first tourism installations (through the Gaviota hotels chain), dollar stores, and other foreign currency–generating enterprises.[87] Cuba claimed that tourist visits increased from 400,000 in 1991 to 600,000 in 1993, with gross revenues of $530 million.

Concerns about emerging income disparities and loss of state control over the economy led to the national assembly imposing restrictions on self-employment in December 1993. Decree 141 was amended to favor cooperatives over individual businessmen; 140 categories of permitted self-employment were limited to repair shops, certain kinds of restaurants, and taxi drivers, and they were taxed at 49.9 percent.

Despite these restrictions, the very modest economic reforms succeeded in stabilizing Cuba's economy and enabled a modest recovery. Several senior officials—including economy czar Carlos Lage Dávila,

---

[85] Banco Central de Cuba, 1998, p. 15.

[86] Edward Gonzalez and David Ronfeldt, *Storm Warnings for Cuba*, Santa Monica, Calif.: RAND Corporation, MR-452-OSD, 1994, pp. 14–15.

[87] Gonzalez and Ronfeldt, 1994, p. 23.

finance minister José Luis Rodríguez García, and foreign minister Roberto Robaina González—quietly pushed for additional economic reforms and met with visiting journalists to aggressively tout oil exploration leases, Cuba's biotech industry, and tourism. Castro gave a series of interviews to prominent U.S. news media outlets as part of a charm offensive during the Bill Clinton administration, arguing for lifting of the U.S. embargo. The raft exodus crisis in 1994 revealed the depth of discontent and desperation; tens of thousands of Cubans set sail for Florida in rickety contraptions. This discontent led to a reimposition of central control over the economy. The outflow prompted the Clinton administration to detain migrants in Guantanamo Bay detention camp and then on U.S. bases in Panama. The influence of reformist officials was eventually curtailed when Robaina was dismissed as foreign minister on corruption charges and others were eased out of their positions.

No Political Opening Amid Increasing U.S. Pressure

During this period of Cuba's principal economic reform and opening of its economy, European and Canadian governments responded with expanded trade and investment, but they coupled their overtures with calls for political liberalization and support for human rights activists. In 1996, the European Union adopted a "Common Position" to influence political liberalization and improve Cuba's human rights record through engagement rather than through economic embargo as the United States had done. By 2001, the European Union was Cuba's largest trade partner (it was subsequently surpassed by Venezuela in 2002) and remained Cuba's largest export market and largest source of FDI; it also accounted for roughly half of the tourists visiting Cuba in the 1990s.[88] In 2003, the European Union adopted economic sanctions following the jailing of 75 political dissidents in Cuba.

During the 1990s, the U.S. government passed two significant pieces of legislation: the Cuba Democracy Act and the Helms-Burton "Libertad" bill, which aimed to squeeze the regime and bring about political liberalization. The regime reacted predictably by circling the

---

88 Council on Hemispheric Affairs, "The European Union and Cuba: The Common Position," July 15, 2010.

wagons in a repeat of the cycle of mutual hostility that had characterized the bilateral relationship since the 1960s.

A variety of factors account for the lack of political liberalization in Cuba. The regime's Soviet bloc–trained security and intelligence services maintained a tight grip on the population. Although revolutionary fervor waned dramatically and fewer citizens participated in watchdog activities (such as the Committees for the Defense of the Revolution) or the Communist Party, the regime used jobs, access to foreign currency, permission to travel abroad, and other means of control to suppress dissent. In the early decades of the revolution, U.S. hostility shored up popular support for the revolution and Cuban nationalism generally, but the immigration policies of the United States served as a significant escape valve for Cuban discontent. The Cuban Adjustment Act of 1966 granted legal residency to Cubans who arrived in the United States. During the massive raft exodus crisis of the mid-1990s, migrants were housed offshore in an effort to stem the flow without altering this policy. The Clinton administration eventually granted a waiver permitting those Cuban migrants to come to the United States.

The course of events in the former Soviet Union (particularly Russia) also served a cautionary function for Cuban leaders. The fates of Gorbachev and Boris Yeltsin did not encourage Cuba to follow perestroika or glasnost, and the advent of populist and leftist governments in Latin America in the 2000s provided a community of like-minded regional leaders. Although only Venezuela and Brazil were in a position to provide substantial material support, other friendly governments in Ecuador, Bolivia, Argentina, Uruguay, and Nicaragua reduced Cuba's sense of isolation.

Raúl Castro Ruz's Accession and Further Reform in the 2000s

The collapse of the Soviet Union in the 1990s induced the first major period of changes in the Cuban system. The second wave of changes occurred after the ailing Fidel Castro passed the reins of power to his brother informally in 2006, a move that was formalized in 2008 with the election of Raúl Castro Ruz to president of the Council of State.

From 2004 to 2007, Cuba enjoyed the first real surge of economic growth since the collapse of the Soviet bloc, with growth averaging 9 percent in these years. The global financial crisis and a series of storms caused a downturn in subsequent years, averaging 2.8 percent growth from 2011 to 2015. In 2008, the European Union provided a five-year package of development aid because relations had improved after the release of 14 political prisoners in 2005. After the release of 52 prisoners in 2010, the European Union renewed multiyear assistance in 2014.

In this same period, the United States took several steps to increase U.S.–Cuban exchanges across various areas. In 2000, the U.S. Congress passed the Trade Sanctions Reform and Export Enhancement Act of 2000, which authorized certain sales of food, medicines, and medical equipment to several countries, including Cuba.[89] Those exports peaked in 2008, when Cuba began importing more from the European Union and Brazil. In 2009, Congress passed an appropriations measure that eased restrictions on family travel and travel for the marketing of agricultural exports.[90]

In 2009, the Obama administration took further unilateral steps to change Treasury Department Office of Foreign Asset Conroll regulations to permit family travel and family remittances to Cuba and in 2011 to permit nonfamily remittances and educational and religious travel to the island.

In April 2011, Raúl Castro Ruz made his mark by introducing important economic reforms at the 6th Party Congress, such as permission for Cubans to buy and sell real estate and cars, reduction of party oversight of state firms, a plan to move 20 percent of the island's five million state employees to the private sector, reduction of government oversight of the economy, and increased taxation. These moves to separate party and state functions and allow greater economic autonomy were coupled with the introduction of term limits and rotation in leadership posts.[91]

---

89 Public Law 106-387, Agriculture, Rural Development, Food and Drug Administration Appropriations Act, October 28, 2000.

90 Public Law 111-8, Omnibus Appropriations Act, March 11, 2009.

91 Eusebio Mujal-León, "Survival, Adaptation and Uncertainty: The Case of Cuba," *Journal of International Affairs*, Vol. 65, No. 1, Fall/Winter 2011.

In 2010–2011, the Catholic Church facilitated the release of 125 political prisoners; another 53 prisoners were released as part of the U.S.–Cuban normalization of relations in 2015 (although some of those would be rearrested). The Cuban government appeared to make a policy shift toward short-term detentions in these years, possibly to achieve the desired domestic political effects without suffering the international opprobrium that long-term detentions had incurred.

Obama's Opening to Cuba

President Obama's moves to loosen restrictions on travel and remittances made clear his desire to seek normalization of relations with Cuba. Legislation limited what he could do without the support of Congress. Only Congress could lift the embargo, which was the one change Cuba sought above all else. Nonetheless, the Obama administration's normalization of diplomatic relations in July 2015 marked a significant historic watershed in U.S.–Cuban relations.

The first overture was made at the funeral of South African leader Nelson Mandela in December 2013, when Obama shook Raúl Castro Ruz's hand in full view of the crowd and international cameras. A series of back-channel meetings occurred with various intermediaries, notably Pope Francis and the Cuban cardinal, Jaime Ortega.[92] Two of Obama's White House aides went to Canada to meet secretly with Raúl's son Alejandro, leaving official diplomats sidelined until the deal was struck.[93] The release of Alan Gross, a U.S. aid worker imprisoned in Cuba, was a necessary condition for a deal. A parallel spy swap was arranged for Cuba to secure the release of the final three members of the "Cuban Five," who had been sentenced and jailed for espionage in the United States.

In December 2014, just after the U.S. Congress recessed, the swap was made, and the Obama administration announced its inten-

---

92 Ruadhán Mac Cormaic, "Cardinal's Secret U.S. Visit Paved Way for Obama-Castro Détente," *Irish Times*, March 16, 2017; Katharine Q. Seelye, "Cardinal Jaime Ortega, a Cuban Bridge to the U.S., Dies at 82," *New York Times*, July 26, 2019.

93 A senior U.S. diplomat surmised that secret talks were underway when one of the aides consulted him on various points (telephone interview with Jeffrey DeLaurentis, March 18, 2019).

tion to restore diplomatic ties, remove Cuba from the official list of state sponsors of terrorism, and seek further exchanges with the island. Technical talks ensued, Cuba was removed from the list in April 2015, diplomatic relations were formally restored in July 2015, and U.S. commercial flights to Cuba began in August. A series of regulatory changes were made to allow further commercial activity and exchanges, such as the opening of mail, travel, and receiving offices in Cuba. In March 2016, Obama traveled to Havana with his family, where they were greeted by enthusiastic crowds lining the streets.

The 7th Party Congress and the Advent of the Trump Administration

Following the historic U.S. presidential visit and the announcement of restoration of diplomatic relations without any major concessions on Cuba's part, one might have expected Raúl Castro Ruz to be triumphal in his appearance before the Party Congress in April 2016. However, a public rebuke from his brother, a biting editorial in the Cuban Communist Party–controlled daily *Granma*, and the traditional use of the Party Congress to reaffirm the communist liturgy prompted him to offer a pugnacious conclusion to his own speech, making a series of demands that the United States lift the economic embargo, cease its democracy promotion programs in Cuba, return the naval base at Guantanamo, and stop pressuring fellow leftist Latin American governments with what he called "unconventional warfare." Reprising the suspicious stance that the Cuban regime has often adopted toward the United States, he added "There are more than a few U.S. government officials who, on recognizing the failure of their policy toward Cuba, make no attempt to disguise their affirmations that the goals remain the same, only the means are being modified."[94]

The election of Trump as U.S. president in November 2016 set in motion a policy review that resulted in a June directive reversing some of the opening that the Obama administration had begun, but flights and cruise visits continued. In September 2017, Hurricane Irma caused severe damage to Cuba, reducing economic growth. The downturn

---

[94] "7th PCC Central Report, Presented by First Secretary Raúl Castro Ruz," transcript, CubaDebate, April 18, 2016.

was compounded in 2018 when Brazil announced that it would suspend a medical services agreement that provided $400 million annually to Cuba for medical professional services provided by Cuban doctors in Brazil.

As of 2019, Cuba faced serious countertrends, as Venezuela's crisis deepened with the imposition of U.S. sanctions on the government in Caracas. Some U.S. officials, including members of Congress, appeared ready to extend the campaign of pressure from ousting President Nicolás Maduro Moros to forcing further change in Cuba. The historic pattern of stiffening resistance within Cuba could repeat itself, precluding the desired opening.

The economic changes instituted by Raúl Castro Ruz and the slow but inevitable passing of the revolutionary generation appear likely to transform Cuba more thoroughly over time.[95] The loosening of state controls over Cubans has unleashed entrepreneurial energy, although the existence of a dual currency system and other constraints limit the effects. Increased travel; access to the internet, cell phones, and computers; and cultural and educational exchanges have limited the Party's control over Cuban society despite the official policy of maintaining a one-party political system.[96] The Cuban regime remains afraid of the consequences of rapid economic change and prefers to meter its reforms lest it lose control.

Factors That Influenced North Korea's Past Economic Reforms

In recent years, DPRK government pronouncements have placed heavy emphasis on economic development, and some observers say that Pyongyang might undertake substantial economic reform initia-

[95] Richard E. Feinberg, *Open for Business: Building the New Cuban Economy*, Washington, D.C.: Brookings Institution Press, 2016.

[96] Carmelo Mesa-Lago, "The Emerging Non-State Sector in Cuba's Economy," *Latin American Research Review*, Vol. 52, No. 1, July 2017; Grace Stainback, "Exploring the Cultural and Infrastructural Impacts of Consumerism on the New Cuba," *Hatfield Graduate Journal of Public Affairs*, Vol. 3, No. 1, 2018.

tives in the future.[97] To understand the prospects of any such reforms, an understanding of the economic reform measures the country has undertaken in the past and the motivations for these could provide valuable insights into the DPRK leadership's thinking.

From the end of the Korean War until the 1970s, North Korea achieved respectable economic growth through a centrally planned economic approach that focused on armaments, infrastructure, and heavy industry that was facilitated by substantial aid and technical advice from the Soviet Union and China. In the 1970s, however, the economy began to stagnate as it reached the inherent limitations of a socialist economic system.[98] After defaulting on and refusing to pay back its international debt obligations in the 1970s,[99] the economy remained sluggish into the early 1980s. In a bid to extract further resources from the international community, the DPRK government enacted a law in 1984 designed to attract FDI; this was not, however, enough to lure substantial additional funds.[100] From 1984 to 1989, only 100 contracts were made; 70 of them were from Korean-Japanese businessmen and only ten were from Western businesses. Out of 100, only 53 investments were actually implemented and few were profitable because of North Korea's bureaucracy and lack of business infrastructure.

North Korea's economy continued to decline throughout the 1980s. In 1991, with the collapse of the Soviet Union (which had been North Korea's principal trading partner and source of aid), the

---

97 It is important to note that North Korea does not permit its officials to describe its economic initiatives using the language of "reform" and routinely pillories the notion of applying the word itself to any DPRK economic policies. See Adrian Buzo, *Politics and Leadership in North Korea*, 2nd ed., New York: Routledge, 2017.

98 As happened in the other socialist countries, the DPRK economy started stagnating, mainly as a result of inefficient planning and decreased productivity from lack of motivation and innovation. See Paul Hare, "North Korea: Building the Institutions to Raise Living Standards," *International Economic Journal*, Vol. 26, No. 3, September 2012.

99 Kim Youngnam, "N. Korean Debt to Sweden Remains Unpaid After Four Decades," Voice of America, October 26, 2017.

100 Besides the 1984 law, North Korea did not undertake any market-oriented reforms until the 1991 Rajin-Sonbong SEZ was initiated. In comparison, China implemented broader economic reforms beginning in the late 1970s.

country's economy began to grind to a halt. Following Moscow's 1990 lead, China recognized South Korea in 1992 and informed the DPRK regime that it would be reducing food, fuel, and other subventions and would require future payments to be made in hard currency. North Korea has rarely produced sufficient sustenance for its population, and DPRK leaders' unwillingness to open up in reaction to these external developments resulted in a disastrous famine in the mid-1990s, during which between 1 and 3 million North Koreans are estimated to have perished.[101] DPRK leaders favor economic developments that they can control, and they direct the benefits to the elite cadre. This type of benefit to a class of people can aid in managing support for the Kim family and others in the leadership circle. Engaging in broader economic activity involving free market activities and international trade is more difficult to control and might stimulate economic and political forces that the regime could not control.

Despite the regime's clear need for an alternative economic growth model, Kim Il-Sung undertook few steps toward economic reform prior to his death in 1994. Shortly thereafter, the country entered a prolonged period of food scarcity because of the lack of agricultural output.[102] During the famine, which the regime dubbed "the Arduous March," the DPRK government did little to address its domestic food shortage beyond requesting international aid. Pyongyang blamed its food shortages on flooding and drought, but it took no steps to open up as a way of staving off widespread food shortages. As food disappeared, the public distribution system largely broke down, and unofficial markets sprang up as the people started trading for food. The government's control over the population weakened because it could not control people's movements as they left their towns searching for food. Furthermore, the government could not enforce regulations as effectively as people could avoid them by bribing bureaucrats. The unof-

---

[101] Stephan M. Haggard and Marcus Noland, "North Korea's External Economic Relations," Peterson Institute of International Economics Working Paper No. 07-7, August 2007. Also see Andrew S. Natsios, *The Great North Korean Famine: Famine, Politics, and Foreign Policy*, Washington, D.C.: U.S. Institute of Peace Press, 2001.

[102] The most substantial step, the establishment of the Rajin-Sonbong Free Trade Zone, is discussed in this report's subsection on SEZs.

ficial market activities that emerged during this period continue in the present day.

Since the famine, the DPRK government has intermittently experimented with two basic types of economic reforms: regulatory reforms and the establishment of SEZs. Regulatory reforms were intended either to incorporate unofficial market activities into the official system or to deter (or reverse) spontaneous growth of market activities. The government's goals in these cases were not to introduce a market economy but to regain control over the economic system for the state and quash private-sector economic activity. This a key difference from when China and Vietnam engaged in economic reform that led to broad economic growth and in limited efforts designed to garner economic benefits for SOEs or ventures controlled by an elite cadre. The DPRK government's attempts were met with broad evasion and were largely unsuccessful, though they did damage economic productivity. The regime's establishment of SEZs appears more like an attempt to establish a market economy. Although North Korea has experimented with multiple forms of SEZs since the establishment of the Rajin-Sonbong SEZ in 1991, these efforts, with the notable exceptions of the Mt. Kumgang tourism program and the Kaesong Industrial Zone, have not been successful in bringing in much foreign investment. The following section examines these in more depth.

North Korea's Post-Famine Economic Reforms

July 1, 2002, Reforms

The government enacted another economic reform in 2002, but the goal was to recognize officially the changes already happening in the market rather than to improve the economy. On July 1, 2002, the government increased product prices and labor wages comparable to the prevalent unofficial market prices. The price of rice, for example, was increased from 0.8 won/kg to 40 won/kg.[103] Before the economic crisis, such low prices allowed the government to provide necessities to the people almost for free. During the famine, the government had no way

[103] Christopher D. Hale, "Real Reform in North Korea? The Aftermath of the July 2002 Economic Measures," *Asian Survey*, Vol. 45, No. 6, 2005.

to incentivize production, had little to distribute, and therefore was unable to provide necessities. Many people left the cooperative farms or the state-owned factories and started farming in whatever lands they could use and working in the unofficial markets. In these unofficial markets, prices were set by demand and supply, and the scarce food and necessities were traded at much higher prices. To bring back the people to the farms and factories, the government had to pay higher prices and salaries. Additionally, to reflect the prevalent market rate, the government adjusted the official foreign exchange rate from 2.15 won/dollar to 150 won/dollar.[104] After the reform, market prices continued to rise, diverging again from the official prices, and the public distribution system never recovered.

Pyongyang also gave more autonomy to SOEs. Because the government could no longer provide subsidies to them, it required them to source their own raw materials and cover their own costs of production. With this step, it also allowed them to make some business decisions, such as what types of products to produce and how many—as long as they could meet production quotas. (In addition to quotas, the government also retained power over personnel decisions, such as hiring and firing.) Reportedly, some government-owned restaurants and stores transitioned to a type of semi-recognized private ownership at this time. These private parties could own their businesses by paying a rent and dividing profits with the government.[105] Because the regime was focused on survival and largely incapable of operating factories and restaurants, authorities largely tolerated these measures as a way to extract resources from society in the form of bribes and protection money.

In contrast to policies in the areas of pricing, labor, and private-sector firms, the government conducted a market-oriented agricultural experiment in which it implemented a "land-lease" program in two cities in the Hampyong province. In this program, farmers leased plots from what were previously collective farms and kept a certain por-

[104] Hale, 2005.

[105] Hale, 2005.

tion of the produce.[106] It appears that while trying to restore the ration system, the regime also sought to experiment with Chinese-style agricultural reform. North Korea implemented a fully extended agricultural reform in 2012 (see that subsection for more details).

In summary, these reforms allowed those affected—enterprise managers, business owners, and some farmers—to trade in markets and capture profits. Though largely reactive, these reforms exposed the overall economy to market supply and demand signals to a limited extent.

2002–2009 Reforms

Following the July 1, 2002, reforms, the DPRK government implemented measures that were largely inconsistent and detrimental to the economy, most of them aimed at recovering the regime's control over the economy. For example, in 2002, the DPRK government announced that the euro, not the U.S. dollar, would be the official foreign currency against which the won would be benchmarked, although the general population continued using dollars in the unofficial markets.[107] In 2003, some unofficial farmers' markets were transformed into official markets, but these were not attractive for the traders because market prices were higher in the unofficial markets; also, the unofficial markets (although not legitimate) were still protected by the bribed officials.[108] In 2005, the government banned the sale of rice in the official markets, but this led to broad resistance.[109] The government also tried to reduce market activities with an aim of eradicating all such activities by the late 2000s. For example, in 2007, the government announced

---

[106] In the previous system, farmers had to sell all their produce to the government at set prices and buy their food through the official system at the subsidized prices.

[107] Jae-Cheon Lim, "Institutional Change in North Korean Economic Development Since 1984: The Competition Between Hegemonic and Non-Hegemonic Rules and Norms," *Pacific Affairs*, Vol. 82, No. 1, Spring 2009.

[108] Tat Yan Kong, "The Political Obstacles to Economic Reform in North Korea: The Ultra Cautious Strategy in Comparative Perspective," *Pacific Review*, Vol. 27, No. 1, 2014.

[109] Eun-Lee Joung, "North Korea's Economic Policy as a Duet with Control and Relaxation: Dynamics Arising from the Development of Public Markets Since the North Korean Famines in the 1990s," *Journal of Asian Public Policy*, Vol. 9, No. 1, 2016.

a ban on women under age 40 trading in the markets but then failed to compel the enforcement.[110] In 2009, the government enacted a currency reform with a week's notice that required all holders of DPRK won to convert their currency into a newly issued version at punitive rates, destroying much of the privately held wealth in the country while sucking some assets into the government's coffers. This caused massive confusion and hurt the economy badly; it also caused many DPRK elites to distrust the financial system and hoard foreign currencies.[111] After the currency reform, North Korea had an economic depression and did not enact any further major reforms until 2012.

The June 28, 2012, and May 30, 2014, Reforms

After assuming power in late 2011, Kim Jong-Un enacted two major reforms in 2012 and 2014. These reforms aimed at increasing productivity and efficiency by decentralizing economic decisionmaking, reducing the government's role in such decisionmaking, and incentivizing productivity through profit-sharing. Companies were given almost full autonomy; managers could make business plans and day-to-day decisions and were also permitted to determine wages for labor. With this, labor income could be differentiated according to productivity and skill. In agriculture, farmers were broken into small groups of five to eight people, each of which was given land for cultivation and full autonomy over production decisions, with output split with the government. In 2012, the farmers' share was set at 30 percent (70 percent to the government), a figure that was increased to 60 percent in 2014 (with 40 percent to government).[112] The government also moved to decontrol some prices while still setting others for certain key products.[113] The government also redefined its role from direct, detailed planning to a more removed role in setting an overall strategy.

[110] Lim, 2009; Kong, 2014.

[111] Kong, 2014.

[112] Chung H. Lee, "A Study of the DPRK's Economic Policy Through the Seventh Party Convention" (in Korean), *Review of North Korean Studies*, Vol. 19, No. 3, 2016.

[113] Lee, 2016.

SEZs

Since the 1980s, the DPRK government has sought to attract foreign capital; at the same time, fearing the loss of control, the regime has tended to establish SEZs where FDIs and market economy rules were permitted but also hived off from the rest of the country.

Rajin-Sonbong SEZ, 1991–Present

In 1991, North Korea established an SEZ in the Rajin-Sonbong region to attract FDI from capitalist countries. However, the SEZ was largely unsuccessful and most of the investment went into service sector businesses, such as hotels, casinos, and restaurants. In 2010, the DPRK government designated Rajin as a special city and signed a US$10 billion project with the Chinese government.[114] Under the plan, the Chinese government acquired 50-year use rights for the three piers at the port. China subsequently repaired the Rajin port and built logistics warehouses. China also rebuilt the highways and a bridge connecting the country to Rajin. Russia also joined the project, agreeing to forgive 90 percent of North Korea's debt and pledging US$300 million in additional investments. Russia repaired the railways connecting Rajin to Russia's Khasan city, and trains started running in 2013. Russia also repaired one of Rajin's piers to handle 4 to 5 million tons of goods.[115] However, these projects stalled after Kim turned on his uncle (who was leading the project), purging and executing Jang Song-Thaek in late 2013.[116] During their 2018 summits, Kim and Chinese leader Xi Jinping reportedly discussed reinstating the Rajin development.[117]

---

[114] Under the Belt and Road Initiative, the Chinese government wants to develop the Rajin port to export products from China's northeastern region; Rajin is attractive to China because it is a warm water port that does not freeze during the winter and thus could provide year-round access to the Pacific Ocean.

[115] B. H. Cho, *North Korea's Special Economic Zone Development Trend and Inter-Korean Cooperation* (북한의 경제특구 개발 동향과 남북협력 연계방안), Seoul: Korea Development Institute, September 2014.

[116] Kim's uncle-in-law Jang was executed in December 2013. One accusation was that he was trying to sell national property to a foreign country.

[117] Multiple Korean news outlets reported that they discussed development of North Korea's SEZs. See, for example, Choi Ik-Jae (최익재), "Kim Jong-Un Demands Xi Jinping to Negotiate

The Sinuiju Special Administrative Region, 2002

In 2002, North Korea announced that Sinuiju, which sits on the border with the Chinese city of Dandong, would henceforth be designated as a Special Administrative Region. The city was reportedly to be given full autonomy, with its own legal system and administration, and Yang Bin, a Dutch citizen of Chinese origin, was to be appointed as a governor. The project was abruptly halted when Yang was arrested by the Chinese authorities for tax evasion.[118] Kim appears to be keen on developing the region. In 2013, the DPRK government announced 14 SEZs, including Sinuiju.[119] In 2014, North Korea allegedly signed a deal with a Hong Kong–based conglomerate to develop Sinuiju, and after Yang was released from his full term in 2018, he was reportedly looking to reestablish his business ties with North Korea.[120] It is also reported that Kim discussed Sinuiju development with Xi during their 2018 summit and that Kim visited the region late last year.[121]

The Kaesong Industrial Complex, 2002

In 2002, Kaesong municipality was designated an industrial region, with North and South Korea agreeing to develop it as an industrial park at which Republic of Korea (ROK) firms could employ DPRK labor in producing goods for export. Hyundai, a major ROK conglomerate, led the land development, and the park started its operation in 2005 with 15 ROK companies. By 2015, the number of ROK businesses had grown to 125, employing an estimated 55,000 North Koreans and manufac-

---

with Four North Korean Bases (김정은, 시진핑에 북한 4대 거점 경협 요구)," *JoongAng Ilbo* (중앙일보), June 6, 2018.

118 Hale, 2005.

119 Y. H. Kim, "Kim Jong-Un Administration's Economic Reform Evaluation for the Second Year in Power (집권 2년차, 김정은 정권의 경제개혁 평가)," *KDI North Korea Economic Review* (KDI 북한경제리뷰), March 2014.

120 "N. Korean, Hong Kong Firms to Develop Border City of Sinuiju," Yonhap News Agency, March 12, 2014; Katsuji Nakazawa, "Chinese Billionaire Who Plotted with North Korea Pops Up After 16 Years," *Nikkei Asian Review*, October 25, 2018.

121 "North Korea's Central Broadcaster: 'Kim Jong-Un Inspects Sinuiju and Maps Construction Plans' (북한 중앙방송 "김정은, 신의주 시찰하고 건설계획 지도)," Maekyung Economics, November 16, 2018.

turing US$563 million worth of products annually, roughly 50 percent of which were textiles.[122] Nevertheless, ROK businesses suffered from North Korea's arbitrary policies, especially two sudden closings induced by spiking inter-Korean political tensions. In 2009, North Korea unilaterally announced that it was scrapping the agreed-on wage and rent agreements that it had with ROK firms and went on to demand wage increases.[123] In 2012, North Korea demanded that additional taxes be paid by some companies.[124] In 2013, North Korea blocked ROK access to the region and pulled out DPRK laborers, eventually leading to a complete shutdown. Although the Kaesong facilities were reopened later that year, the ROK government shut down the park in 2016 in protest of DPRK nuclear tests. (It remains closed at present.)[125] Kim suggested reopening the Kaesong industrial park in his 2019 New Year's remarks.[126]

The Wonsan–Mount Kumgang Special Tourist Zone, 2002

In 1998, ROK tourists first started visiting Mt. Kumgang, and in 2002, the DPRK government designated the region as a special tourist zone. Hyundai led the development of Mt. Kumgang. In July 2008, a 53-year-old ROK tourist was shot dead by a DPRK soldier after she wandered off the tour route and into what Pyongyang described as "a military area." Tours of Mt. Kumgang were suspended and then ceased altogether by the ROK government.[127] In his 2019 New Year's remarks, Kim suggested reopening the tourist zone.

---

[122] Kaesong Industrial District Management Committee, homepage, undated.

[123] "N. Korea Withdraws Demand for Steep Wage Hike at Joint Park," Yonhap News Agency, September 11, 2009.

[124] Yonhap News Agency, "S. Korean Firms in Gaeseong Complex Plagued by North's Hefty Taxes," *Korea Times*, October 18, 2012.

[125] "Kaesong Talks: North and South Korea Reach Agreement," BBC, July 7, 2013.

[126] Michael R. Gordon and Andrew Jeong, "Kim Jong Un Extends Peace Overture to U.S.," *Wall Street Journal*, January 1, 2019.

[127] Jon Herskowitz and Kim Junghyun, "South Korean Tourist Shot Dead by North Soldier," Reuters, July 11, 2008.

Hwanggumpyong and Wihwa Islands Free Trade Zone and Other Development Zones

In 2011, the DPRK and Chinese governments announced an agreement to develop the islands of Hwanggumpyong and Wihwa at the mouth of the Yalu River (adjacent to Dandong and Sinuiju) into a free trade zone focused on four sectors: information, tourism, agriculture, and light industry. China was to build roads, ports, and electrical and internet networks. The project was stopped shortly after Jang was executed in 2013. Allegedly, the development of this region was discussed during the Kim-Xi summit. After their third summit in 2018, Kim visited the region.[128]

Additionally, from 2013 to 2015, a total of 21 additional regions were designated as economic development zones, with 17 additionally designated as "regional" economic development zones. For these regional zones, the government purportedly drew up economic development plans designed to take advantage of regional strengths and comparative advantages. The government reportedly was actively developing relevant laws for these up until 2015.[129]

Understanding DPRK Motivations for Economic Reform

What motivated DPRK leaders over the past 35 years to pursue the various economic reform initiatives described in the previous sections? Was the regime attempting, if unsuccessfully, to move away from central planning and toward a market economy? Or were DPRK leaders motivated by other goals?

Kim Il-Sung certainly did not undertake economic reforms to move toward a market economy. Despite widespread evidence on his watch of North Korea's economic decline, South Korea's economic boom, the Soviet Union's collapse, and China's rise, his only two reform initiatives were the 1984 FDI law and the establishment of the

---

[128] Kim Da-Hye (김다혜), "Kim Jong-Un Visited Pyeongbuk-Sindo-Gun on the Border with China (김정은 방중 후 첫 행보는 중국접경 평북 신도군 시찰)," News1, June 30, 2018.

[129] J. H. Hong, *North Korean Economy in the Kim Jong-Un Regime for 5 Years: Focusing on Economic Policy* (김정은 정권 5년의 북한경제: 경제정책을 중심으로), Seoul: Korea Institute for National Unification, 2017.

Rajin-Sonbong SEZ in 1991.[130] He implemented no other economic reform initiatives, nor was he focused on raising living standards or adjusting his economic plans in light of their failure.[131]

Kim Jong-Il similarly does not appear to have undertaken any of his economic reform initiatives to fundamentally shift the basis of the DPRK economy in the direction of greater openness or reliance on markets. Despite some initial hopeful analyses suggesting that his 2002 reform would open the system up, those measures were intended not to adopt a market economy so much as to rebuild the official ration system by positioning it to better compete with the market and reestablish control over the population. Similarly, the government permitted the companies some autonomy not because they wanted to incentivize the managers (and thereby increase productivity) but because the government could not provide raw materials and was, in essence, making a virtue of necessity. Between 2005 and 2008, Pyongyang took a series of steps intended to *reverse* the growth of market activities. Although these countermeasures largely failed, they nonetheless indicated the regime's deep interest under Kim Jong-Il in preserving control at the expense of economic growth. Kim Jong-Il differed from Kim Il-Sung in his greater openness to foreign capital, though this might simply have been a function of the regime's greater desperation in the wake of the Soviet collapse and China's reduction in assistance.

Kim Jong-Un's economic reforms, though still limited, appear to be more market-oriented than those of either his grandfather or his father. In agriculture, for example, farmers are now allowed to retain up to 60 percent of their produce. Similarly, the government gave companies full autonomy to incentivize the managers and thereby increase productivity. Moreover, unlike his father, whose key policy line was "military first" (*son'gun*), Kim Jong-Un has made it clear that his national priority is "dual advance" (*byungjin*), or simultaneous emphasis on the buildup of

---

130 The Rajin-Sonbong Special Economic Zone was established in 1991 (before Kim Il-Sung died in 1994). However, this might have been Kim Jong-Il's initiative: Although officially he assumed power only after his father's death, he had taken over much of the day-to-day running of the country by the early 1980s.

131 Buzo, 2017.

the country's nuclear arsenal and the achievement of economic development; more recently, Pyongyang has proclaimed that the development of its nuclear and ballistic missile arsenals is basically complete, so attention can now shift more fully to economic construction.

If Kim Jong-Un decides to undertake major economic reforms, several factors from the regime's past might shape the way he goes about doing so. For example, unofficial market activities have become fundamental to the overall DPRK economy. In 2000, the unofficial market economy was estimated to account for between 25 percent and 50 percent of the total economy.[132] Today, the DPRK government literally could not operate without the money flowing from the unofficial markets. There is a symbiotic relationship between the DPRK government and the unofficial markets that works at both individual and organizational levels. Because government officials cannot live on their low official salaries, they accept bribes to allow market activities and/or trade on such markets. Because the government cannot fund the national projects, it receives investments from private investors (*donju*).[133] Kim likely knows that if he tries to repudiate market development, government operations will also be disrupted.

Moreover, according to some analyses, North Korea is experiencing a shift in its core power elite, witnessing a rising generation of young, second-generation offspring of high officials who have profited from illicit trade and from their families' roles in key SOEs.[134] Such elites might be Kim's nucleus of supporters, and they are likely to want

---

[132] Andrei Lankov, "The New Leader, The New Economic Model," in William H. Overholt, ed., *North Korea: Peace? Nuclear War?* Cambridge, Mass.: Mossavar-Rahmani Center for Business and Government, 2019.

[133] The market activities created a new entrepreneur-investor class called *donju* ("master of money") that amassed significant wealth through the market. Members of this class have become owners of the businesses and investors in many of the government businesses. They provide bribes to the government officials and share the profits with the governments. Under Kim Jong-Un's leadership, *donju* are encouraged to invest in government projects and SOEs. See Lankov, 2019.

[134] "Interfering with Various Interests of the North Korean Version of the 'President' and Taking Bribes (북한판 '태자당' 각종 이권 개입하며 뇌물 받아)," Voice of America (미국의 소리), December 1, 2010.

the economy to continue to develop so they can amass wealth.[135] Kim also likely calculates that achieving a certain level of economic growth and stability is required to maintain domestic political stability.

Therefore, Kim's pathway to any reforms might be strewn with substantial internal obstacles resulting from past economic steps. Vested interests might oppose true opening up that would deprive them of the chance to earn rents (trading on their privileged access to resources and markets). North Korea's past efforts to engage in limited, tactical economic reforms have also laid down a marker that will lead many to regard Kim with skepticism, including people he needs to believe in his leadership and reform efforts, which means he will have to expend additional resources to build credibility if he wants reforms to actually launch and take hold.

Conclusions

As demonstrated by this review of economic reform decisionmaking in communist regimes, the factors that tend to stand out when it comes to economic policy change appear to correlate highly among these regimes' calculations about what they need to do to stay in power. When famines have broken out in China and North Korea, the regimes have weathered these without dramatically changing their policies; for Vietnam, however, when the emergence of large-scale hunger appeared likely to lead to major societal resistance to the regime in Hanoi, VCP leaders opted to relax their grip on the economy to encourage growth. In all cases, reform only took place when powerful leaders who were opposed to economic liberalization died or were eased aside. In the cases of Cuba and North Korea, even the loss of a great-power patron who provided enormous ideological and/or material resources was not enough to spur change. However, such a loss did provide a more permissive environment in Vietnam for the VCP to adopt economic reform policies in a context of eroding government finances and con-

---

[135] They are known to enjoy lavish consumption and the Western lifestyle. See Anna Fifield, "North Korea's One-Percenters Savor Life in 'Pyonghattan,'" *Washington Post*, May 14, 2016.

trol over the economy, the emergence of hunger, and the rise of a new generation in the wake of Le Duan's death. Similar situations occurred in Cuba and (to a limited extent) in North Korea.

Although these findings are preliminary and based on a limited number of case studies, they nonetheless suggest that it is unlikely that Pyongyang will adopt a radically new policy direction overnight absent a very dramatic forcing event. Some recent analyses have suggested that the sanctions regime has been beginning to show increasing effect, although (as noted at the outset) such external pressures are often mediated by intervening variables, such as the reaction to sanctions pressures by politically important elites and their expectations of the DPRK leadership.[136] Pyongyang's increasing need to replace lost revenues explains the pressure on officials posted abroad to generate funds to support the regime, spurring a wave of reported defections and disappearances and prompting the regime to recall many of its key diplomats for ideological and loyalty screening.[137]

Under such circumstances, despite Kim's claim to be abandoning *byungjin* in favor of a single-minded focus on economic development, it seems likely that his administration will pursue its own tradition of tactical or unwilling informal opening up, followed by a reimposition of control at the earliest opportunity. In so doing, the Kim regime would be both following in the footsteps of Cuba and drawing on its own past experiences.

We conclude that the cases studied here do have several factors in common, although no single factor emerges as the sole predictor of a communist regime's decision to open up its economy to free markets, foreign investment, and more international trade (Table 2.1).

These factors include, most notably, a rapid deterioration in central government finances, a relaxation in the necessity for ideological purity (linked in the cases of Vietnam and Cuba to prior decisions by

---

[136] Joshua Stanton, "The 'Experts' Were Wrong. The Sanctions Are Working," *Free Korea*, April 23, 2019.

[137] Lukas Mikelionis, "North Korea's Top Diplomat in Italy Defected, Embarrassing Kim Jong Un," Fox News, January 3, 2019; Julian Ryall, "North Korea Recalls Diplomats to Undergo 'Ideological Examinations' After Embarrassing Defections," *The Telegraph*, March 29, 2019.

Table 2.1
Factors Shaping Communist Economic Reform Initiative Decisions

Factor	China	Vietnam	Cuba	North Korea
Removal of leader opposed to opening	X	X	X	
Scarcity of food and consumer goods	X	X	X	X
Hyperinflation		X		
Loss of foreign aid and patronage		X	X	X
Economic sanctions		X	X	X
Expansion of illicit markets		X		X
Declining central government finances	X	X	X	X
Loosening ideology	X	X	X	

China and the Soviet Union to pursue economic liberalization, thus providing Hanoi and Havana with a measure of political cover)—and, most important, the removal from office or death of key leaders who had opposed reform. Other factors also affect reform decisions, such as incipient famine and widespread demands for improvement in living conditions that threaten to shake the regime's grip on power, spreading corruption and the erosion of control over the state-led sector of the economy, and/or the loss of a great-power patron.

The policies of the United States in either encouraging these regimes to open up or sanctioning them for their foreign policies or domestic abuses does not appear to have figured directly in most of these instances of communist reform decisionmaking. Most of these governments were under some degree of economic pressure from the United States and continued to have challenging relationships with Washington, but their decisions to reform do not appear to be a direct outgrowth of either U.S. threats to impose harsher sanctions or U.S. offers of assistance if the regimes move toward economic liberalization. The United States certainly should continue to use carrots and sticks in an attempt to move North Korea toward a new approach to governing, economic development, and the conduct of its foreign relations, but the effects of such incentives are likely to be felt somewhat indirectly and to work only if the Kim regime perceives that it is facing a situation in which U.S.-led sanctions are putting its continued survival at risk.

CHAPTER THREE

Conventional Deterrence on the Korean Peninsula: Two Scenarios for Analysis

Some key historical elements have shaped the integrity of deterrence on the Korean Peninsula. On June 26, 1950, in the early morning hours, the DPRK Army launched a large ground offensive across the 38th parallel into South Korea. North Korea's aim was to quickly destroy the fragile ROK Army standing in its way as it moved south to unite the two Koreas under its control. Unfortunately for the North Koreans, the United States moved Japan-based ground forces with air support onto the Peninsula in early July, which ultimately stopped the DPRK Army and eventually evicted it from all of South Korea.[1]

The lesson that the North Koreans drew from that experience that still resonates today is that if they want to have freedom of action—whether political or military—the most optimal condition is to keep

[1] See Allan Millet, *The War For Korea: They Came from the North*, Lawrence, Kan.: University Press of Kansas, 2010; and Roy E. Appleman, *South to the Naktong, North to the Yalu, June 1950–November 1950*, Washington, D.C.: Center of Military History, 1961. For a recent historiographical survey of Korean War literature, see James I. Matray, "Korea's War at 60: A Survey of the Literature," *Cold War History*, Vol. 11, No. 1, February 2011; James F. Schnabel and Robert J. Watson, *History of the Joint Chiefs of Staff*, Vol. III, *The Joint Chiefs of Staff and National Policy, 1950–1951, The Korean War, Part 1*, Washington, D.C.: Office of Joint History, Office of the Chairman of the Joint Chiefs of Staff, 1998; Walter G. Hermes, *Truce Tent to Fighting Front*, Washington, D.C., Center of Military History, 1966; Morton Halperin, Peter Hayes, Thomas Pickering, Leon Sigal, and Philip Yun, "From Enemies to Security Partners: Pathways to Denuclearization in Korea," Nautilus Peace and Security Network Net Policy Forum, July 6, 2018; Tim Shorrock, "Can the United Nations Command Become a Catalyst for Change on the Korean Peninsula?" *National Interest*, November 1, 2018; and Shawn Patrick Creamer, "The United Nations Command and Sending States," unpublished monograph, undated.

U.S. forces off the Korean Peninsula—or, at a minimum, keep the United States from reinforcing the forces that are already there.

Since the Korean War ended in 1953, the ROK military—along with the United States and the military forces it has deployed to the Korean Peninsula—has maintained a generally conventional deterrence posture that has prevented North Korea from trying to repeat what it attempted in summer 1950. But that does not mean conventional deterrence on the Peninsula has not been tested over the years. Recent examples of conventional deterrence being tested are North Korea's sinking of the ROK Navy ship *Cheonon* in March 2010, North Korea's artillery bombardment of Yeon Pyong Island eight months after that, and skirmishes in May and June 2014 associated with the Northern Limit Line.[2] In each of these cases, the North Koreans walked up to the line but always seemed willing to back down. Conventional deterrence seems to have kept the situation from escalating.

What factors affect DPRK thinking and decisionmaking about conventional deterrence and escalation on the Korean Peninsula? This chapter outlines two plausible future scenarios based on currently available information. These scenarios inevitably entail some speculation about the future with the intent of stimulating discussion about how things might evolve in the future. They are not designed to predict the future; rather, the objective of this exploratory approach is to identify gaps in information that might stimulate new collection requirements, revisiting information collected in the past and encouraging exploratory "what if" thinking. Following a brief discussion of the background for the two scenarios, we present two scenarios in the year 2022 in which conventional deterrence erodes and fails. The scenarios are designed to explore the critical factors that could affect the thinking of Kim and senior DPRK officials during an evolving crisis and what might lead North Korea to attack ROK and U.S. forces stationed on the Peninsula.

---

2 James Pearson and Ju-min Park, "The War That Never Ends Between the Koreas," Reuters, June 16, 2014.

The Two Scenarios

Before laying out the two scenarios, we note the Road to War we used on both scenarios. The idea that Kim would order an outright offensive or military strikes into South Korea is unlikely when relations on the Korean Peninsula are relatively stable or even if there are some tensions between the regime, South Korea, and the United States. Instead, for North Korea to launch military strikes or an offensive, there probably needs to be a provocation cycle that is robust enough to lead the DPRK regime to embrace the risk of starting a war. The Road to War used in both scenarios aims to do just this. In this chapter, we focus on security conditions in South Korea (Scenario 1: "Weaker ROK Army") and on the ROK alliance with the United States (Scenario 2: "Combined Forces Command [CFC] in Trouble") as key factors influencing the integrity of conventional deterrence. Thus, the Road to War is kept intentionally short so that more time can be spent on the conditions surrounding the erosion of conventional deterrence.

The first scenario is centered on ROK President Moon Jae-In's 2018 defense policy that aimed to reorient the ROK military over the following five to seven years toward high-tech weaponry in the ROK Navy and Air Force. In Moon's vision for ROK defense and security policy, the ROK Army would accept cutbacks in funding, which would reduce the total number of ROK Army combat divisions, and, importantly, lessen the conscription period for ROK males from 22 months to 18. The Moon administration's shift in ROK defense policy also contains a significant change in the primary threat posed to South Korea—away from North Korea as the primary threat and toward regional competitors, such as China and Japan. As a result of these changes in ROK defense and security policy projected into a future scenario in 2022, Kim and North Korea might sense a weakening of South Korea's conventional military capabilities.

In the second scenario, conventional military deterrence for South Korea weakens in a different way. Unlike in the first scenario, which is premised on the recent Moon administration defense reforms, the advantage that North Korea sees in 2022 in the second scenario stems from a strategic shift in the security relationship between the

United States and South Korea. As projected in this scenario, both the U.S. and ROK governments agree to abolish the longstanding U.S.-led United Nations Command (UNC) and CFC. Thus, where a U.S. four-star general had been in command of the UNC since 1952 and the CFC since 1978, in 2022, a U.S. three-star general would be in command only of U.S. forces in South Korea. This shift occurs because U.S. foreign policy becomes stridently isolationist with the reelection of President Trump. In this second scenario, Kim and DPRK leadership perceive a weakened U.S.-ROK alliance, thus providing an opportunity to advance militarily.

The two scenarios posit that a DPRK perception, real or mistaken, of weakened U.S.-ROK deterrence will lead to erosion of conventional deterrence. Each scenario ends with North Korea carrying out military action, but it does not consider the next steps that might occur. The purpose of ending the scenarios in this way is to generate discussion on what happens when a crisis occurs in which conventional military power is used, conventional deterrence erodes, and escalation to the use of nuclear weapons becomes a possibility. Finally, to inform the following two scenarios, it is useful to keep in mind how North Korea might perceive the following factors or conditions:

- DPRK perception of the military threats from South Korea or the United States or from other regional actors in terms of their capabilities and disposition of forces
- DPRK internal regime dynamics
- Third-party intervention by key regional actors, such as the United States, China, Japan, or Russia
- DPRK perception of an opportunity to use military force to further its objectives
- DPRK understanding of chemical weapons as part of its conventional deterrent
- the strength of the U.S.-ROK alliance.

These factors can shape and affect how North Korea perceives (rightly or wrongly) a weakening in conventional military deterrence on the Korean Peninsula and, in turn, how it might act on those perceptions.

Scenario 1: Moon Defense Reforms Erode Conventional Deterrence

By the start of 2022, the defense reforms put in place by former ROK President Moon in 2018 have had profound effects on the entire ROK military, especially the ROK Army. Although the ROK Air Force and Navy saw increased investments in modernization in high-tech weapon systems and associated sensors, the ROK Army has really felt the effect of the Moon reforms.[3] The logic for the Moon reforms was that South Korea needed to boost the technological capabilities of its air force and navy because they could play a bigger role in safeguarding ROK interests from potential threats from regional actors other than North Korea. The assumption is that South Korea needs to curb Chinese and Japanese threats to its interests in the region.

One impact of the Moon military policy changes is the goal to reduce the overall manpower end strength of the ROK Army by about 15 percent. The implication of this policy change is that the downsizing led to the ROK Army's end strength in 2020 being a mere 300,000—a cut of almost 30 percent. This reduction in manpower has had an important effect in the overall number of combat infantry divisions in the ROK Army, going from 16 in 2018 to only nine in 2022. Along similar lines, the total number of ROK Army armored-mechanized divisions, which would provide the offensive punch for any ROK Army operations on the Korean Peninsula, dropped from six in 2018 to only two in 2022.[4]

The sharp reduction in ROK armored-mechanized divisions results partly from the reduction of the conscription period from

---

3 Yeo Jun-suk, "Moon Administration Seeks to Cut Service Period to 18 Months," *Korea Herald*, May 3, 2018.

4 See Josh Smith, "Buying a Big Stick: South Korea's Military Spending Has North Korea Worried," Reuters, September 10, 2019; Sungyoung Jang, "How Will 'Defense Reform 2.0' Change South Korea's Defense?" *The Diplomat*, August 27, 2018; Song Sang-ho, "Defense Reform Plan to Cut Generals, Create Ground Command, Retain 3-Axis System," Yonhap News Agency, July 27, 2019; James M. Minich, *The North Korean's People's Army: Origins and Current Tactics*, Annapolis, Md.: Naval Institute Press, 2005; and Republic of Korea, *2016 Defense White Paper*, Seoul: Ministry of National Defense, May 2017.

21.5 months to only 18. The time required to train an ROK recruit on basic light infantry skills and tactics takes much less time than it takes to train a recruit to become proficient on, for example, a main battle tank, such as the ROK K-1. It simply takes much longer to develop the skill set required for an armored crewman than it does to train a soldier to shoot a rifle and perform relatively simply light infantry tactics. Thus, by 2022, the ROK armored divisions cannot man all six divisions; instead, divisions are reduced to two and manned with ROK noncommissioned officers and soldiers who volunteered to do a three-year enlisted stint.

During the years of the Moon reforms, the ROK administration justified the downsizing of the ROK Army by positing that the DPRK military no longer posed a direct security threat as it had in previous years, which meant that the ROK Army size and capabilities could be cut back. The administration also argued that even if North Korea did remain a threat, albeit a lessened one, the high-tech weaponry improvements of the ROK Air Force and Navy could easily deal with any military provocations put forward by North Korea.

Unfortunately for the Moon administration, its projection that diplomatic relations with North Korea would get better took a significant turn for the worse. Kim had hoped that the fruits of his friendship with President Trump would produce a loosening of economic sanctions against his country, but that did not pan out. As a result, Kim has begun intercontinental ballistic missile (ICBM) testing again in 2022, along with setting off a seventh nuclear test, this one with a high mega-tonnage outcome that put it well within the thermonuclear realm. These aggressive actions occur in tandem with the U.S. administration taking a much firmer, belligerent line with the DPRK regime. Thus, even though the ROK defense policy had reoriented toward a defanged ROK Army by 2022, a very different diplomatic tack has taken place.

In late 2022, amid these rising tensions, an unfortunate event began a provocation cycle that ultimately led to a conventional military confrontation on the Korean Peninsula. A Korean Air flight departed out of Busan bound for Beijing. In its commonly used flight path, it flew about five miles south of the demilitarized zone (DMZ), then turned west toward its destination in China. However, a mistake in navigation took the aircraft to only one mile south of the DMZ. The pilots quickly assessed their error and reasoned that there was no foul because they had not crossed into North Korea. Unfortunately, the DPRK air defense did not see it that way, because U.S. B-52 bombers had been carrying out threatening training flights over the past year that put them on the exact same flight path as the Korean Air civilian airliner. The DPRK air defense radar mistakenly placed that airliner as crossing the DMZ; therefore, the airliner was shot down, killing everyone on board.[5]

The ROK response was quick and lethal. The new ROK president decided to send a strong message to Kim that this kind of behavior would have consequences. By order of the President, the ROK military launched 20 missiles into North Korea: half aimed at one of Kim's personal residences on the outskirts of Pyongyang and the other half at a DPRK air defense command center on the eastern coast near Wonju. At the time of the strike, Kim was visiting a nuclear testing facility in the northern part of the country. When notified, he quickly moved to a command center near Pyongyang and conferred with his military leaders about what the response would be.

After a daylong discussion of his options, Kim decided to carry out a conventional military strike by DPRK ground forces into South Korea. Kim and his key military leaders perceived a vulnerability in the weakened state of ROK ground forces along the DMZ. Thus, over the next two days, DPRK conventional artillery fired a barrage from the western edge of the country along the DMZ east to the Chorwon Valley at ROK population centers south of the DMZ, with the intention of terrorizing ROK civilian population centers, causing panic and evacuations, and thus focusing ROK military response on silencing

---

5 This Road to War modifies the scenario in a novel on a future nuclear war with North Korea: Jeffrey Lewis, *The 2020 Commission Report on the North Korean Nuclear Attacks Against the United States: A Speculative Novel*, New York: Mariner Books, 2018. Also see James Rosone and Miranda Watson, *Battlefield Korea*, Book Two of the Red Storm Rising Series, Grand Rapids, Mich.: Front Line Publishing, 2017; and Vann H. Van Diepen and Daniel R. Depetris, "Putting North Korea's New Short-Range Missiles into Perspective," *38 North*, September 5, 2019.

DPRK conventional artillery. With the ROK Army's focus on DPRK artillery and on assisting in the medical treatment and evacuation of ROK civilians, North Korea then launched a three-division assault across the DMZ and about 10 kilometers into South Korea. The goal of this assault was to seize three key population centers—Paju, Yeocheon, and Chorwon—and, in effect, hold them hostage as a negotiating device to force the ROK government to cease its military strikes.

A twist that further complicated the situation for the ROK government and the United States was that the Chinese Army massed three People's Liberation Army mechanized corps along the Yalu River, its border with North Korea. China's political leaders warned the ROK and U.S. governments that any ground assault into North Korea would bring about a massive Chinese intervention into the conflict.

In this scenario, conventional military deterrence that the U.S.-ROK alliance was supposed to provide eroded to the point at which that weakened deterrence convinced Kim that, in a provocation cycle between North Korea and ROK, he could launch powerful but still limited ground operations and seize a handful of ROK population centers close to the DMZ.

Scenario 2: Changes in U.S.-ROK Command Structures Erode

In this second scenario, the year is 2022 and the heady days of positive diplomatic relations between the U.S. administration and Kim ended with North Korea resuming nuclear weapon and missile tests. A provocation cycle occurs that is shaped by a set of aggressive U.S. bomber "training" flights aimed at intimidating Kim and other DPRK senior officials. North Korea shoots down an ROK civilian airliner; South Korea responds with cruise missile strikes; and North Korea responds with conventional military action.

But Kim's rationale for North Korea's conventional military response in this provocation cycle is different from what it was in Scenario 1. Here, North Korea perceives a weakening in ROK conventional defense because of key decisions make between 2020 and 2021 that removed the U.S. four-star general in his or her dual role as commander UNC and commander CFC. One of the key components of the UNC–CFC command structure since 1978 has been that, during peacetime, a senior ROK general has operational control over ROK military forces and the UNC commander controls the DMZ, as stipulated in the 1953 Armistice Agreement. In wartime, however, operational control over all ROK military forces shifts to the U.S. four-star UNC–CFC commander. The purpose for that wartime control was to ensure a strong alliance between South Korea and the United States by having ultimate command in wartime go to the U.S. commander.[6]

By the mid-1990s, some ROK political and military leaders started to argue that the UNC–CFC command structure was a relic of the past, given the increased capabilities and size of the ROK military. In 2010, a tentative agreement was made between the ROK and U.S. governments to shift all operational-level command in wartime to the ROK military. In 2015, however, both governments decided to push that decision to a later date, largely because of the rise of Kim and his pursuit of nuclear weaponry.[7]

Because the relationship between North and South Korea vacillated between cooperative and antagonistic, the Moon administration in 2021 began to push hard for a shift in command structure to happen sooner rather than later. The core issue for President Moon and his subsequent successor was ROK sovereignty. If South Korea was a strong and independent nation-state with a highly sophisticated military, then why did it need to subordinate its authority over its military forces in wartime to a U.S. commander?

At the same time, U.S. foreign policy became stridently isolationist, reducing U.S. military presence around the world. In this situation, the Moon administration's push for terminating the UNC–CFC command structure hit a positive chord with the United States.

---

[6] For an excellent history of the UNC command during the Korea War, see Shawn P. Creamer, *Answering the Korea Question: U.S. Government Policy Toward the Unified Command and the Korean Armistice Agreement*, Carlisle, Pa.: U.S. Army War College, Civilian Research Project, March 2017.

[7] Sub Kwak Kwang, *The US-ROK Alliance, 1953–2001, Alliance Institutionalization*, Ann Arbor, Mich.: Michigan University Press, 2006.

Thus, the U.S. and ROK governments at the end of 2021 decided to remove the U.S. four-star command, turning it over to an ROK four-star commander. A three-star U.S. Army commander remained in South Korea but only had authority over U.S. forces (in peacetime and in wartime). Both sides argued that it made sense because of the lessening of the DPRK threat and South Korea's new strategic focus on regional threats other than North Korea. Nonetheless, both sides also claimed that the alliance between two countries was as strong as ever and North Korea or any other regional actor should think twice about challenging that alliance.

This shift was something North Korea sought for decades because it guaranteed that any alliance training exercise would be decided on by the ROK government and not in conjunction with the United States. The other enticing element for North Korea about the shift was that it left a U.S. three-star commander in charge of the remaining U.S. forces on the Korean Peninsula without any command links to operational control of ROK forces. For North Koreans who watch the U.S.-ROK military alliance, this change might signal the first step in a general loosening of the alliance and a weakening of the military capabilities North Korea might face in a conflict.

Once the provocation cycle began (the way it did in Scenario 1), Kim and North Korea again perceived a weakness in the conventional warfighting capabilities of the ROK military, this time because of the removal of the U.S. four-star UNC–CFC commander. As a result, Kim sensed an opportunity to use limited DPRK military strikes to force a complete withdrawal of all U.S. forces from South Korea. After discussing his options with his senior military leaders, Kim ordered the use of the regime's array of improved short- to medium-range missiles and its improved multiple rocket launchers to strike the U.S. Army base at Pyeongtaek, the U.S. Navy Headquarters at Busan, and the ROK regional civilian airport at Gimpo.

Kim's thinking in this scenario was that by striking these targets, he could coerce the ROK government onto a path toward unification without U.S. involvement.

Conclusions

An important insight from these two scenarios is that conventional deterrence that has been effective since 1953 could quickly erode during a crisis, given other factors that influence the integrity of deterrence on the Korean Peninsula. Assessing some plausible scenarios in which conventional deterrence is stressed on the Peninsula shows how a stable alignment can be upset by conventional conflict in response to a crisis and quickly escalate to a nuclear crisis. Once fighting with conventional weapons begins, there might be few off-ramps for avoiding a nuclear exchange. A recent study identified four significant challenges that complicate the Korean security situation.[8] First, North Korea's nuclear capability presents a fundamentally different security challenge. Second, North Korea has increased its artillery capability to hold key ROK urban areas at risk. Third, it is virtually impossible to evacuate Chinese, U.S., and other foreign citizens from South Korea in the face of impending conflict. And fourth, fears of DPRK regime collapse could occur with little warning with many potential consequences, most of them bad. Thus, understanding how conventional deterrence works, and how it might fail, is important to understanding nuclear deterrence.

The United States and South Korea can increase the "firebreaks" leading to a nuclear crisis by addressing some of the factors that might influence North Korean perceptions of conventional deterrence on the Korean Peninsula. For example, effectively managing the U.S.-ROK alliance is critical to show North Korea that there are not good options to use military force to achieve its objectives. As part of this management, taking measures to strengthen the alliance's conventional deterrence posture is important. Additionally, states in the region reassuring North Korea that third-party military intervention is unlikely (unless it takes aggressive military action toward South Korea or other states) might constructively influence its perception of threats to the regime.

---

8 Gian Gentile, Yvonne K. Crane, Dan Madden, Timothy M. Bonds, Bruce W. Bennett, Michael J. Mazarr, and Andrew Scobell, *Four Problems on the Korean Peninsula: North Korea's Expanding Nuclear Capabilities Drive a Complex Set of Problems*, Santa Monica, Calif.: RAND Corporation, TL-271-A, 2019.

CHAPTER FOUR

North Korea Nuclear Doctrine

There are some key questions about North Korea's approach to nuclear weapons:

- How does North Korea think about its nuclear doctrine, desired force posture and related capabilities needs, the relationship between its nuclear and conventional forces, and the role of nuclear weapons in deterrence and escalation?
- Under what conditions would North Korea be tempted to consider nuclear use?

In this chapter, we evaluate such key questions by examining open-source data on possible DPRK nuclear doctrines and comparing them with scenarios that might call for the use of nuclear weapons. The result is necessarily somewhat speculative, both because our knowledge of North Korea's nuclear doctrine is extremely limited and because the actual response of national leaders in any given contingency cannot be predicted. Therefore, the analysis in this chapter is designed not to produce concrete findings or predictions but to provide a more-general guide that can help in assessing possible risks and patterns of DPRK behavior.[1]

We start by examining the possible nuclear doctrines that states can choose from and where North Korea might fit, how we can infer DPRK intentions from its official statements, and potential DPRK nuclear doctrines and nuclear use scenarios.

---

1 Gentile et al., 2019.

Nuclear Doctrine: The Range of Possibilities

Any state has a range of nuclear doctrines to choose from, depending partly on technical capacities, threat perceptions, geopolitical context, formal alliances, and other factors. A review of the literature on deterrence—and of the actual deterrence policies of the established nuclear powers—points to several possible approaches to deterrence, including the following:

- *Virtual deterrence:* Deterrence by ambiguity. States deter by intentionally not disclosing, or at least not fully disclosing, their capabilities and/or the conditions under which they would use nuclear weapons[2]
- *Minimum deterrence:* Deterrence by acquiring the smallest possible number of nuclear weapons that could credibly be viewed as sufficient for deterrence. Because of their small number, minimum deterrents are typically postured for retaliation against countervalue targets.[3] States with minimum deterrents do seek to make them survivable, but only to the degree required to promise a minimal, countervalue second strike.
- *Assured deterrence:* Deterrence by acquiring a substantial and secure second-strike capability, one that threatens any attacker with comprehensive retaliation and national destruction beyond the level of a minimum deterrent. Typically, countries that pursue such a policy deploy hundreds of survivable and diverse nuclear weapons across a nuclear dyad or triad.[4] Countries with assured destruction policies can (and often do) still create a strong firebreak between conventional and nuclear war, including such declaratory policies as a no-first-use pledge.

---

[2] Zafar Khan, *Pakistan's Nuclear Policy: A Minimum Credible Deterrence*, Abingdon, UK: Routledge, 2015, p. 3.

[3] Khan, 2015, p. 7.

[4] Vipin Narang, "Nuclear Strategies of Emerging Nuclear Powers: North Korea and Iran," *Washington Quarterly*, Vol. 38, No. 1, Spring 2015.

- *Asymmetric deterrence:* The most risk-acceptant of deterrence approaches, typically chosen by states that have extraordinarily intense threat perceptions. A state deters by integrating nuclear weapons into its warfighting strategy and threatens to escalate very readily from a conventional conflict to a nuclear one. States pursuing such strategies typically deploy a variety of nuclear weapons from low to high yield to create multiple escalatory options.

These approaches are not mutually exclusive. A state can pursue both minimum and asymmetric deterrence, for example, deploying a small arsenal with countervalue retaliatory policies but tightly integrated with conventional warfighting capabilities and designed to threaten rapid escalation. Nuclear powers have typically combined elements of multiple deterrence strategies: The United States employed aspects of assured and asymmetric deterrence; China, France, and the United Kingdom have largely employed minimum deterrence strategies but with the growing hallmarks of assured deterrence. Some analysts say that Pakistan has an asymmetric strategy and that Russia has integrated some aspects of asymmetric strategy into recent statements on nuclear use doctrines.

Available evidence seems to suggest that North Korea aspires to achieve capabilities consistent with both assured and asymmetric deterrence.[5] The variety and character of nuclear systems that North Korea has pursued speak, at a minimum, to a perceived need for a level of assured deterrence through mobile land-based missiles and missile-firing submarines. At the same time, it appears to be prepared to blur the line between conventional and nuclear use—as a product of its perception of conventional inferiority—in ways that speak to an asymmetric deterrent strategy.

Some observers (including senior-level participants in recent RAND wargames on DPRK nuclear-use scenarios) sometimes contend that North Korea would not use nuclear weapons until the endgame of a conflict because it would realize that the response would be devas-

---

[5] A good discussion of this is in Sung Chull Kim, "North Korea's Nuclear Doctrine and Revisionist Strategy," in Kim and Michael D. Cohen, eds., *North Korea and Nuclear Weapons: Entering the New Era of Deterrence*, Washington, D.C.: Georgetown University Press, 2017, pp. 35–36.

tating. But there are countervailing pressures: North Korea's strategic situation means that it would almost certainly feel pressure to strike first on the brink, or in the early stages of, a future war, partly out of a concern for its vulnerability and perhaps in the hope of forcing an early conflict termination. As Vipin Narang has argued:

> Faced with the prospect of a U.S.-led invasion, Pyongyang's conventional inferiority requires it to degrade the United States' ability to sustain the attack against it. This means it essentially has no option but to use nuclear weapons first against targets such as Andersen Air Force Base in Guam, which stations American bombers, and a variety of allied bases in Japan and South Korea.[6]

In practice, North Korea does have options short of nuclear use to disrupt U.S. force flow and military operations, but most observers agree that they would constitute holding actions at best. And North Korea's perception of its susceptibility to a U.S. first strike could create significant crisis instability; as Narang, 2017, concludes, "States with small arsenals that are put under counterforce pressure have itchy trigger fingers."

For these and other reasons, North Korea might look to Pakistan as a possible model for developing a nuclear force and accompanying use doctrine. Like North Korea, Pakistan faces a primary adversary with conventional superiority. It also could face multiple adversaries at the time same (in Pakistan's conception, India and, in some extreme scenarios, the United States). Its security relationship with China is close, but to a degree that it can count on Beijing for a reliable security guarantee. Additionally, Pakistan engages in asymmetric provocation attacks against its main rival, as does North Korea, and values the ultimate deterrent that nuclear weapons could provide as a cover for such activities.

In sum, then, the experience of other nuclear powers points to several overarching nuclear strategies and deployment approaches that North Korea might adopt. These still would not prescribe situations in which nuclear weapons would be used, but they would provide broad guidance about the role of those weapons in national strategy.

---

6 Vipin Narang, "Why Kim Jong Un Wouldn't Be Irrational to Use a Nuclear Weapon First," *Washington Post*, September 8, 2017.

Inferring Intentions: DPRK Official Statements

The regime's official statements provide a second source of information on North Korea's evolving nuclear doctrine. DPRK official state media can often provide clues to the regime's beliefs and strategies—or at least to what DPRK leaders *want* the world to think—because the messages are so tightly controlled.[7] Pyongyang's official statements have offered clues about its possible nuclear doctrine. Official statements, Alexandre Mansourov has explained, have "alluded to the fact that the North Korean government has already developed a set of standard operating procedures for the authorization of the employment of nuclear weapons in wartime."[8] Those signals point to a concept for the role of nuclear weapons that is increasingly elaborate and risk-acceptant.

The spring of 2013 seems to have been an important moment in North Korea's public references to the role of nuclear weapons. Kim declared the emergence of a "new strategic line" marrying nuclear capabilities with enhanced economic performance at home, the so-called *byungjin* policy.[9] North Korea published a law governing nuclear

---

7 One challenge in inferring DPRK doctrine from government statements or leaders' behavior is that states can have divergent views on nuclear doctrine and broadcast conflicting or misleading signals. Writing on the DPRK case, Peter Hayes and Scott Bruce point out that there is frequently a divergence "between what a country's leaders say and what its nuclear war planners and military units do," and they argue that "nuclear weapons organizations are complex entities that often distort outcomes intended by high-level decisionmakers, or lead to perverse, unintended actions that are invisible to those at the top" (Peter Hayes and Scott Bruce, "Translating North Korea's Nuclear Threats into Constrained Operational Reality," in Gregory Moore, ed., *North Korean Nuclear Operationality*, Baltimore, Md.: Johns Hopkins University Press, 2014, pp. 17, 29). Declaratory policy is not always the best clue to a country's real doctrine or ultimate behavior. This problem might be somewhat attenuated in a totalitarian system in which all officials will be looking closely to the ultimate leader's statements for guidance. But caution should be taken in drawing simple lines between public statements and nuclear use practices.

8 Alexandre Mansourov, *Kim Jong Un's Nuclear Doctrine and Strategy: What Everyone Needs to Know*, Berkeley, Calif.: Nautilus Institute for Security and Sustainability, Nautilus Peace and Security Special Reports, December 16, 2014.

9 Hong Yung Lee, "North Korea in 2013: Economy, Executions, and Nuclear Brinkmanship," *Asian Survey*, Vol. 54, No. 1, January/February 2014, p. 90. This *byungjin* policy of building nuclear weapons and at the same time advancing economic growth was approved in March 2013. At the same time, Kim Jong-Un himself gave a speech in which he referred to the

weapons at that time, which was accompanied by many public references to threats of nuclear escalation. The Korean Central News Agency (KCNA), for example, broadcast images of Kim reviewing an "operational plan of the KPA [Korean Peoples' Army] Strategic Rocket Force for firepower strike" in March 2013. It was during this period that North Korea claimed that it "exercise[d] the right to launch a preemptive nuclear attack in order to destroy the strongholds of the aggressors." Official DPRK broadcasts have mentioned such targets as Guam, Japan, Hawaii, and a variety of U.S. cities stretching from Los Angeles to Washington, D.C.[10]

That 2013 law, the "Law on Consolidating the Position of Nuclear Weapons State," appears to remain the single most significant and authoritative public DPRK pronouncement on its nuclear doctrine.[11] This generally commits the DPRK regime to developing a nuclear force capable of imposing immense destruction on states that undertake aggression against it; insofar as the law is any guide, the objectives are essentially defensive. The law itself makes no mention of a no-first-use doctrine, suggesting that North Korea views conventional and nuclear operations as part of an unbroken continuum (though such a no-first-use policy, or something like it, has come up in other DPRK official statements). The notion of an "unbroken continuum" is obfuscated by North Korea's 2013 "Law on Consolidating Position of Nuclear Weapons State," which states that nuclear weapons are for defensive purposes.[12]

DPRK official statements have highlighted several specific components of a possible nuclear doctrine to serve the objectives of the

---

"pivotal role of nuclear weapons in war-deterrent strategy and war-waging strategy." The official DPRK national security strategy states that "the nuclear deterrent enables peaceful development at home" and protects the state ("2013 Plenary Meeting of WPK Central Committee and 7th Session of Supreme People's Assembly," North Korean Economy Watch, April 1, 2013).

[10] Cited in Hong Yung Lee, 2014, pp. 91–92.

[11] Daniel Wertz, Matthew McGrath, and Scott LaFoy, "North Korea's Nuclear Weapons Program," National Committee on North Korea, April 2018.

[12] KCNA, "Law on Consolidating Position of Nuclear Weapons State Adopted," April 1, 2013b.

state. North Korea's most-essential state objectives begin with deterring U.S. aggression, and its doctrine presumably has this as a fundamental and guiding goal. Many DPRK statements emphasize that its nuclear arsenal is a product of U.S. aggressive threats, especially nuclear threats. North Korea claims to be justified in its acquisition of nuclear capabilities because it is operating under coercion.

Increasingly, North Korea has made specific reference to nuclear strikes against the United States, including Washington, D.C., and the White House.[13] Such claims suggest a DPRK ambition to target U.S. bases, and public statements have explicitly mentioned such sites as U.S. facilities in South Korea, Guam, Hawaii, and the western United States. DPRK statements imply that such strikes would be part of an offensive doctrine that aims at the capacity to strike a crippling blow against enemy conventional forces.

North Korea has publicly claimed that nuclear weapons will "beat back any aggressor troops at one strike."[14] Another statement referred to its intention to "desolate the bases of nuclear provocations with our method of merciless preemptive strikes."[15] Kim himself has referred to a plan to "blow up and reduce everything to ashes at a single nuclear strike."[16] Such claims of all-out retaliation might stem from a DPRK belief that it remains vulnerable to nuclear preemption and that piecemeal employment of nuclear weapons might only invite a disarming U.S. attack.

---

[13] KCNA, "Official Statement of the Committee for the Peaceful Reunification of Korea," August 12, 2015b. Also see KCNA, "Official Statement of the National Emergency Measures Committee on Opposition Against Nuclear War Exercises to Invade DPRK," April 23, 2015a; and KCNA, 2013b, which claims that nuclear weapons "serve the purpose of deterring and repelling the aggression and attack of the enemy" by "dealing deadly retaliatory blows at the strongholds of aggression." A more recent statement described a DPRK drill that simulated "preemptive strikes at ports and airfields in the operational theater in South Korea where the U.S. imperialists nuclear war hardware is to be hurled" (KCNA, "Kim Jong Un Guides Drill for Ballistic Rocket Fire," July 20, 2016b).

[14] KCNA, 2013b.

[15] KCNA, 2015a. The same statement contains suggestive references to "a do-or-die battle to provide an epochal occasion" to end the U.S. aggressive threat, again implying a massive, single strike.

[16] Quoted in Mansourov, 2014.

Multiple DPRK official statements and descriptions of some DPRK exercises imply a willingness to preempt expected U.S. military action, whether conventional or nuclear. One 2016 operational scenario, for example, seems to describe a preemptive strike.[17] And in response to U.S. military exercises in 2014, North Korea expanded the scope of nuclear threats to cover limited clashes. If the United States were to "perpetrate a military provocation for igniting a war" in various areas, including "the five islands in the West Sea of Korea" or in the DMZ, "it will not be limited to local war, but develop into an all-out war, a nuclear war."[18]

DPRK statements have been inconsistent on whether North Korea would target South Korea with nuclear weapons, sometimes suggesting that North Korea would refrain from nuclear attacks on fellow Koreans but at other times threatening nuclear decapitation attacks against the ROK government—specifically, strikes on the Blue House.[19]

DPRK public statements suggest that Pyongyang is seeking miniaturization to provide a more flexible range of nuclear employment.[20] Some DPRK public documents have gone so far as to specifically define the goal as nuclear warheads of less than 15 kilotons and have suggested that smaller warheads are more useful because of the level of development of the Korean Peninsula, which makes it difficult to use powerful weapons without causing massive collateral damage. Official statements have also indicated that smaller warheads can make better use of a limited stockpile of fissile material.

Official DPRK statements have referred explicitly to building "various types of nuclear weapons with the aim of successful attain-

---

[17] Léonie Allard, Mathieu Duchâtel, and François Godement, *Pre-Empting Defeat: In Search of North Korea's Nuclear Doctrine*, London: European Council on Foreign Relations, November 22, 2017, p. 3.

[18] KCNA, 2015a.

[19] KCNA, "Crucial Statement of KPA Supreme Command," February 23, 2016a; and Allard et al., 2017, p. 3.

[20] North Korea's public statement on the occasion of its third nuclear test, for example, claimed that it was "conducted with more miniaturized, lightweight, diversified nuclear weapons compared with the former models. . . . The weapons' nuclear yield and other characteristics correspond precisely to their design values" (KCNA, "KCNA Report on a Successful 3rd Underground Nuclear Test," February 12, 2013a).

ment of a wide range of military objectives." These public statements have explicitly distinguished among various categories of weapons, such as strategic, tactical, and battlefield nuclear capabilities. *Strategic weapons* target cities and large military targets; *tactical weapons* target enemy forces in operational areas; *battlefield weapons* have a similar focus but a shorter range. More broadly, there is evidence in DPRK official statements of a growing aggressiveness in elements of doctrine.[21]

Thus, if recent DPRK public statements are any indication, Pyongyang might have elaborate notions of the roles that its nuclear weapons might be able to perform. The statements point to a doctrine well beyond any form of minimum or existential deterrence, one that is designed to create the risk of large-scale and widespread nuclear retaliation, which theoretically could be used as a cover for aggressive actions.[22] These statements and DPRK nuclear development trajectories point to the desire to field an impressive variety of nuclear capabilities that could ensure various first-strike and retaliatory options. There is also a disturbing suggestion that North Korea might be adopting a doctrine of an all-out, comprehensive preemptive blow to be launched when a U.S. attack that threatens regime survival is underway or even anticipated.

But even in DPRK public statements, there is evidence of perceived constraints on the role and use of nuclear weapons.[23] North Korea appears to be aware of several geopolitical problems with unconstrained nuclear capabilities and threats. It has sought to qualify its nuclear aspirations in notable ways, which could create some boundaries to the sorts of doctrine it is willing to embrace. These statements have suggested limits to the appropriate uses of nuclear weapons: In 2006, for example, North Korea appeared to enunciate a no-first-use policy in the wake of a nuclear test (though this has not been consistently reaffirmed). There is also evidence that DPRK leaders since Kim

---

21 See Andrew O'Neil, "North Korea's Changing Nuclear Posture," *The Strategist*, April 17, 2013. See also KCNA, "Question and Answer with President of Nuclear Scientific Research Center," September 15, 2015c.

22 Sung Chull Kim describes the gradually growing ambitions of the DPRK approach to nuclear weapons (Kim, 2019, pp. 37–38).

23 KCNA, 2013b.

Il-Sung have hesitated to target South Korea, for fear of the effect on their intended identity as liberators of their fellow countrymen (as well as perhaps more-practical concerns, such as fallout risks). But North Korea does not make this promise for states that "join a hostile nuclear weapons state in its invasion and attack on the DPRK," which presumably would include South Korea.[24]

Pyongyang also appears to take seriously the significance of the decision for nuclear use and has hinted at command and control (C2) arrangements more rigid and centralized than would be expected for a fully articulated flexible response doctrine. The most significant public statement made so far on nuclear doctrine, for example—the reports surrounding 2013's "Law on Consolidating the Position of Nuclear Weapons State"—specifically claimed that nuclear use could only be approved "by a final order of the Supreme Commander of the Peoples' Army" and that the purpose of the use would be to "repel invasion or attack from a hostile nuclear weapons state and make retaliatory threats." The same document promises to "establish a mechanism and order" for "safekeeping and management so that nukes and their technology, weapon-grade nuclear substance may not leak out illegally."[25]

Along with such obscure declaratory statements, North Korea has solidified its command structures for nuclear deterrence. In 2012, as it revised its constitution to formally declare itself a nuclear state, Pyongyang established the Strategic Rocket Command as an independent entity. Later, it renamed this command the Strategic Rocket Force, then the Strategic Force.[26] It can be assumed that this process has been accompanied by a growing formalization of doctrinal and C2 proce-

---

24 Mansourov, 2014. See also John M. Sanford and Andrew Scobell, *North Korea's Military Threat: Pyongyang's Conventional Forces, Weapons of Mass Destruction, and Ballistic Missiles*, Carlisle, Pa.: Strategic Studies Institute Publications, April 3, 2020, p. 96; and Alexandre Y. Mansourov, "The Origins, Evolution, and Current Politics of the North Korean Nuclear Program," *Nonproliferation Review*, Spring-Summer 1995, p. 30; and KCNA, 2013b, which says that "The DPRK shall neither use nukes against the non-nuclear states nor threaten them with those weapons unless they join a hostile nuclear weapons state in its invasion and attack on the DPRK." This would justify strikes on both South Korea and Japan.

25 KCNA, 2013b.

26 Wertz, McGrath, and LaFoy, 2018.

dures, although evidence of these aspects of North Korea's nuclear development is lacking.

North Korea's recent behavior does not speak, at least so far, to a state determined to use a growing nuclear arsenal combined with a strategy of escalation dominance to engage in increasingly dangerous provocations. Since mid-2013, for example, apart from momentary crises over disputes at the DMZ, North Korea has reverted to a relatively standard, and generally restrained, process of interaction with the United States and South Korea. So far, North Korea's growing arsenal has not produced any straight-line outcomes of growing belligerence.[27]

Potential DPRK Nuclear Doctrines

We can infer a set of possible DPRK doctrines that might fit some combination of evidence. These doctrines might ultimately reflect a middle ground between North Korea's most-extreme aspirations and the realities of the geopolitical situation and the technical constraints inherent in the production of nuclear weapons. Such analysis is necessarily speculative, given the limits of our understanding of DPRK thinking (and even actions).[28] Various observers have examined the same broad set of evidence and come to very different conclusions. Until recently,

---

[27] This accords with some limited but suggestive empirical research indicating that nuclear weapons do not empower regional powers to acquire more in confrontational situations. See Todd S. Sechser and Matthew Fuhrmann, "The Coercive Limits of Nuclear Weapons," paper prepared for the Annual Meeting of the International Studies Association, Montreal, Canada, March 16–19, 2011.

[28] Scobell and Sanford conclude that

> North Korea may or may not possess an explicit doctrine for its nuclear arsenal. Judging from the experience of other states that became nuclear powers, such as China and India, it is quite possible that North Korea has yet to devise one. Lack of attention to formulating a doctrine is plausible especially since the consuming preoccupation almost certainly has been simply to develop nuclear weapons and then build an arsenal. Moreover, even if it has done so, this probably has not been expressed in the form of a written document. (Scobell and Sanford, 2020, p. 87)

Their discussion of the ambiguity doctrine (pp. 88–93) presumes that at least some implicit understandings of the role of nuclear weapons are guiding DPRK nuclear develop-

most experts said that the sum total of incentives for North Korea would encourage it to retain a relatively minimal nuclear posture.[29] Peter Hayes and Scott Bruce, for example, said that North Korea would not be confident of getting nuclear weapons to their targets and therefore would be unlikely to aim for a highly varied, flexible nuclear employment policy. They argue that "the sole use of nuclear weapons in North Korea would be defensive in the context of an all-out war."[30]

Other assessments of DPRK nuclear aspirations found the basis for much more-ambitious nuclear doctrines. Joseph Bermudez argued that, at a minimum, North Korea seems to be moving to assured second-strike capability.[31] Kier Lieber and Daryl Press express concerns about a much more elaborate doctrine of "coercive nuclear escalation."[32] Vipin Narang has said that North Korea's basic objective is a nuclear posture

---

ments and use policy. But these could be very rough, not coherently articulated (or even written down), and might not govern actions in a crisis.

[29] Terence Roehrig, for example, said that future DPRK doctrine is likely to remain in the realm of minimum deterrence, with a few dozen weapons kept in a largely countervalue posture (Terence Roehrig, *North Korea's Nuclear Weapons: Future Strategy and Doctrine*, Cambridge, Mass.: Harvard University Kennedy School, Belfer Center Policy Brief, May 2013). Hayes and Bruce argued that North Korea was likely to adopt a variant of a minimal strategy built largely around using nuclear weapons emplaced in tunnels and other primitive means of disrupting a U.S. or ROK attack (Hayes and Bruce, 2014, pp. 25–26).

[30] Hayes and Bruce, 2014, pp. 27, 29. Andrei Lankov similarly argued that a minimal force is "more than enough for the dual purposes of deterrence and blackmail." A nuclear force ten times as large, he contends, would not increase deterrence or blackmail abilities by a commensurate amount (Andrei Lankov, "North Korea's Nuclear Blackmail," *New York Times*, opinion piece, November 25, 2010). Victor Cha similarly argued that a form of "existential" deterrence, not even extending to an assured second-strike capability, would be sufficient for most of the basic regime-preservation goals (Victor Cha, "North Korea's Weapons of Mass Destruction," *Political Science Quarterly*, Vol. 117, No. 2, Summer 2002, pp. 214–219).

[31] Joseph S. Bermudez, Jr., *North Korea's Development of a Nuclear Weapons Strategy*, Washington, D.C.: U.S.-Korea Institute at the Johns Hopkins School of Advanced International Studies, pp. 13–14. Several DPRK doctrinal options are discussed in Bruce Bechtol, "Planning for the Unthinkable: Countering a North Korean Nuclear Attack and Management of Post-Attack Scenarios," *Korean Journal of Defense Analysis*, Vol. 23, No. 1, March 2011.

[32] Keir A. Lieber and Daryl G. Press, *Coercive Nuclear Campaigns in the 21st Century: Understanding Adversary Incentives and Options for Nuclear Escalation*, Monterey, Calif.: U.S. Naval Postgraduate School, Report 2013-001, March 2013, p. 2.

that "envisions catalyzing third-party military or diplomatic assistance when a state's vital interests are threatened."[33]

For our analysis, we reviewed evidence from DPRK objectives, capabilities, public statements, and the variety of options available to Pyongyang to offer an estimate of the likeliest set of emerging doctrines. These are summarized in Table 4.1.

We distinguished directed, operational forms of nuclear use from the much broader and more-diffuse political roles of nuclear weapons. North Korea has already made clear that its "doctrine" encompasses a broad variety of purposes for nuclear weapons, some operational and some more broadly political and even economic.[34] In North Korea's case, these broader roles feature enhancing regime legitimacy by symbolizing state power and strength, contributing to economic revitalization by offering deterrent power on the cheap and generating resources through blackmail and technology cooperation or sales, and generating competitive advantages in inter-Korean competition. Nuclear weapons also presumably play a significant domestic political role in solidifying Kim Jong-Un's power.

There is significant overlap among several of the doctrines outlined in Table 4.1. For example, the minimum deterrence and catalytic

---

[33] Related to virtual deterrence, a catalytic strategy does not require a large or operationally sophisticated nuclear force, merely one sufficient to create perceived risks of instability that the sponsor power would feel the need to deal with. The critical variable in the Korean case, Narang argues, is China: If North Korea believes China's support to be largely guaranteed, then its nuclear arsenal "can remain limited and recessed." Fears about China's reliability would prompt "an alternative nuclear strategy: an aggressive first-use posture—including developing short-range and tactical nuclear weapons" to guarantee deterrence (Narang, 2015, pp. 74–75).

[34] One source has concluded that "Traditional U.S. deterrence concepts and postures . . . are not well suited to addressing attempts at low-level coercion by secondary nuclear powers with limited conventional capabilities" (Jerry Meyerle, *Nuclear Weapons and Coercive Escalation in Regional Conflicts: Lessons from North Korea and Pakistan*, Arlington, Va.: CNA, November 2014, p. 2). Lieber and Press argue that countries most concerned about losing a conventional conflict to a militarily superior foe—and particularly those regimes that expect their top officials to be prosecuted in the wake of defeat, and ones that worry intensely about domestic uprisings if a war begins to go badly—are the likeliest to adopt coercive doctrines. Their analysis points to North Korea as the single likeliest nuclear state to adopt such doctrines (Lieber and Press, 2013, pp. 26–31, 33–34, 39).

Table 4.1
Potential DPRK Nuclear Doctrines

Doctrine	Minimum Deterrence	Catalytic	Massive Preemption	Assured Retaliation	Asymmetric Escalation
Basic concept	Create existential risk of nuclear escalation to ensure regime survival	Use potential for nuclear development to lock in support from third-party sponsor	Facing attack, launch whole force in one preemptive blow to cripple U.S. power	Threaten survivable second strike to deter nuclear aggression	Multiple nuclear options with various delivery systems; aim for escalation dominance
Targeting policy	Minimal: Often implied or unstated; presumed countervalue	Minimal: Often implied or unstated; presumed countervalue	Extensive: U.S. and allied military bases throughout Asia and, if reachable, continental United States	Flexible: Could be either counterforce or countervalue	Variable: Extensive across range of tactical and strategic targets; some counterforce capabilities
Posture requirements	• Minimal: Handful of weapons, no elaborate delivery systems • Testing of weapons proves potential • C2 systems rudimentary	• Moderate: Same as minimum deterrent but with more signals of additional development to spark sponsor reaction • Basic C2 systems	• Moderate: 20–30 or more warheads and intermediate-range delivery systems of crude accuracy • Proven capabilities in weapons and missiles • Basic C2 systems	• Moderate: Dozens of weapons deployed on survivable platforms; mobile or concealed ICBMs and SLBMs • Complex and survivable C2	• Extensive: Dozens, possibly close to 100 weapons of various types mounted on wide range of delivery systems. • Sophisticated and survivable C2
Possible conditions for nuclear use	Imminent regime collapse or large-scale conventional attack	Regime collapse or conventional attack	U.S. attack in course of conflict or expectation of imminent U.S. attack	Limited or large-scale nuclear strikes; on verge of regime collapse	Multiple, in response to many potential escalation scenarios, some sparked by North Korea

NOTE: SLBM = submarine-launched ballistic missile.

strategies have much in common. Also, the organization of the doctrines does not imply a simple spectrum; elements of flexible response could be added to an otherwise minimum posture, and achieving assured retaliation is in some ways just as demanding (and provocative) as a flexible response posture. In the end, we would expect DPRK doctrine to reflect a combination of some elements from several of these ideal types.

To assess the possible utility of different nuclear doctrines to North Korea, we posited three specific regime objectives for its nuclear force (not necessarily in priority order):

1. bolstering regime strength through prestige, legitimacy, coercive power, and nationalist credibility
2. deterring U.S. coercion or attack
3. in extreme circumstances, supporting offensive operations through escalation dominance, empowering provocation or offensive warfare.

We then assessed the degree to which each nuclear doctrine would meet these three goals. Table 4.2 illustrates our analysis. Green is favorable to North Korea, indicating that the doctrine would serve a given objective; red suggests that the doctrine would not meet that objective. The evaluations shown in Table 4.2 suggest several possible conclusions. One is that if North Korea's state objectives are predominantly defensive, the constraints and risks that apply to more-ambitious doctrines would seem prohibitive. Most doctrines achieve the basic regime goal of deterrence, although, over time, DPRK leaders might come to question whether a vulnerable deterrent force can credibly produce such a result. The doctrines that seem to achieve most objectives with relatively modest constraints are massive preemption and assured retaliation. Moreover, because these are not mutually exclusive, Pyongyang could combine them into a single doctrine, aiming for a survivable retaliatory force under tight centralized control to enhance deterrence and gain the prestige value of an advancing capability but not trusting in the ability to ride out a first strike and thus planning for a spasmodic launch once a full U.S. attack is imminent.

Table 4.2
Requirements of DPRK Nuclear Doctrines

Potential Doctrine	Critical Capabilities Required	Objectives Served[a] 1	2	3	Constraints, Risks, and Costs
Minimum deterrence	• Small number of operational warheads • Primitive but effective delivery means • Reliable but not necessarily survivable C2				• Already achieved • Might be an internal constraint on limitations; bureaucratic pressures to expand force • Perception that doctrine is too weak to deter United States; need more-flexible, survivable forces
Catalytic	• Small number of operational warheads • Primitive but effective delivery means • Potential for significant escalation of program				• Capabilities already achieved • Chinese commitment might be a constraint • Domestic constraint; lack of faith in outside powers • More-limited prestige value
Massive preemption	• Intermediate-range missiles or equivalent delivery systems (e.g., submarines, aircraft) • Reliable warheads of significant yield				• Regional strike requires reliable IRBMs, warheads, and REEVs, none of which might be technically feasible • More-extreme options spark regional reaction
Assured retaliation	• Survivable retaliatory systems (SLBMs, mobile ICBMs, HDBTs) • Delivery systems capable of reliably reaching U.S. or allied targets • Reliable warheads, REEVs • Survivable C2				• Requires all capabilities of preemption *and* survivable systems and C2 • North might never have full faith in survivability of system • Demands distributed C2, which runs against grain of regime

Table 4.2—Continued

Potential Doctrine	Critical Capabilities Required	Objectives Served[a] 1	2	3	Constraints, Risks, and Costs
Asymmetric Escalation	• Survivable retaliatory systems (i.e., SLBMs, mobile ICBMs, HDBTs) • Delivery systems capable of reliably reaching U.S. or allied targets • Reliable warheads, REEVs • Survivable and flexible C2 • Variety of flexible nuclear options, tactical and strategic				• Requires all capabilities of preemption *and* survivable systems and C2 • North might never have full faith in survivability of system • Demands distributed C2, which runs against grain of regime • Opens regime to massive strike once first nuclear attack is conducted

NOTES: Along the stoplight spectrum, dark green is favorable to North Korea, indicating that the doctrine would serve a given objective; red suggests that the doctrine would not meet that objective. HDBT = hard and deeply buried targets; IRBM = intermediate-range ballistic missile; REEV = reentry vehicle.

[a] The three objectives are

1. bolstering regime strength through prestige, legitimacy, coercive power, and nationalist credibility
2. deterring U.S. coercion or attack
3. in extreme circumstances, supporting offensive operations through escalation dominance, empowering provocation or offensive warfare.

In terms of the C2 of nuclear forces, every open-source indication suggests that North Korea's nuclear capabilities have been tightly controlled by a small group at the top of the state hierarchy, dominated by the supreme leader—whether Kim Il-Sung or Kim Jong-Il.[35] The nuclear programs became personally associated with the Kim family, and there is evidence that the Kims were reluctant to delegate any key decisions on the program to the bureaucracy. There is no reliable open-source information on Kim Jong-Un's degree of delegation of nuclear matters. But to the extent that this delegation remains highly centralized, it points to doctrines that do not require extensive and flexible decisionmaking procedures throughout the chain of command. On the other hand, fear of vulnerability could lead to dispersal strategies with predelegated launch authority.[36]

Possible Nuclear Use Scenarios

Using the various sources of evidence we reviewed, we can infer a set of nuclear use scenarios involving North Korea that would reflect the operationalization of these doctrines. The leading objectives of such nuclear use would almost always revolve around a single goal: preserving the regime against actual or feared U.S. (and possibly ROK) military aggression. But that goal can be interpreted in different ways, and North Korea can perceive an imminent threat of U.S. attack where none exists.[37] Even a largely defensive motivation can produce multiple scenarios for possible nuclear escalation. (We also discuss possible offensive motives for nuclear threat or use, although these remain far less plausible— at least for now.)

This analysis also makes clear how much remains intentionally ambiguous—or perhaps actually undecided—in DPRK nuclear doc-

---

35 Mansourov, 1995, p. 29.

36 Meyerle, 2014, p. 16. See also Peter Hayes and Roger Cavazos, "North Korea in 2014: A Fresh Leap Forward Into Thin Air?" *Asian Survey*, Vol. 55, No. 1, January/February 2015, p. 124.

37 See Lewis, 2018.

trine. Many policy choices have simply not been clearly articulated.[38] Despite these significant uncertainties, the combination of factors that we have discussed indicate that the likeliest resting point for the combination of aspirations and constraints regarding the DPRK nuclear arsenal could be a form of general deterrence doctrine combining second-strike potential, somewhat more-varied nuclear capabilities, and an intent to launch an overwhelming strike at the outset of war.

In this context, two scenarios reflect the likeliest situations for the use of nuclear weapons:

- employment of a single warhead, or a small number of them, to achieve very narrow tactical military objectives or larger political signaling goals in the early phases of a conflict, which could include demonstration tests of nuclear weapons associated with delivery vehicles.
- all-out DPRK preemptive nuclear use to forestall imminent defeat or large-scale attack at the hands of U.S. forces.

First Scenario

The first scenario involves a situation in which a conventional campaign on the Korean Peninsula seems about to begin or is underway. North Korea, in this scenario, has not yet made the judgment that the war is escalating to regime-threatening levels. Nonetheless, such an approach might be adopted if Pyongyang begins to sense that the battle is turn-

---

38 As one report concludes,

> Strikingly, the sources do not identify a political endgame to the use of nuclear weapons. They bluff by referring to the destruction of the US, but never discuss the reunification by force of the Korean Peninsula. Missing from the open source material is any evaluation of the consequences of striking the US or its allies with nuclear weapons, or of a clear threshold between a nuclear strike against a military base and a nuclear strike against a city. In sum, North Korea has no clearly defined concept of tactical use of nuclear weapons. . . . In addition, Pyongyang refuses to make a clear choice in its official communications between retaliatory nuclear strikes and deterrence by denial, or to define a sequence of escalation from strikes against military facilities to destruction of cities. In theory, any attack against the country could therefore result in nuclear strikes against military or civilian targets. This looks like an attempt to strengthen deterrence by leaving all options on the table. (Allard, Duchâtel, and Godement, 2017, p. 6)

ing against its forces and that the conventional fight could begin to cascade downhill. It therefore chooses to employ a single nuclear weapon, or just a few, to achieve both local military effects—destroying ROK or U.S. mechanized units, for example, or creating a fallout zone that delays U.S.-ROK operations—and broader signaling goals. Such a limited escalation would be designed to shock the United States into halting offensive operations out of a concern for wider nuclear use by North Korea.

In RAND wargames involving this scenario, North Korea's nuclear use has always unfolded on its own territory. If its goal is a limited escalation, the judgment of RAND players has been that North Korea would realize that to launch significant nuclear strikes on ROK, Japanese, or U.S. territory with massive loss of life would almost guarantee significant retaliation. (This differs from the second scenario, in which North Korea has made the decision to launch a more significant, war-stopping nuclear attack.) This scenario tends to emerge when U.S. or ROK forces have advanced into North Korea and nuclear weapons can be used against them on North Korea's own soil.[39] Given this scenario, North Korea has many employment choices, even preset nuclear "land mines" waiting in expected corridors of advance.

Second Scenario

The second scenario would stem from a DPRK conclusion that the United States was on the verge of an all-out attack on North Korea, either in the form of comprehensive conventional or nuclear strikes or a ground invasion. Such a judgment could emerge during a conflict or even in peacetime (in an analogy to the Soviet paranoia, expressed in Operation Ryan, which produced a conviction that the United States was preparing an out-of-the-blue nuclear strike).[40] North Korea's goal would be to destroy the U.S. potential for power projection against it; the strike would likely feature dozens of nuclear attacks on U.S.

---

[39] In a real circumstance, of course, we cannot know whether North Korea would feel such a constraint. As previously noted, North Korea's statements about its willingness to employ nuclear weapons against South Korea have been inconsistent.

[40] For example, see Nate Jones, "The Soviet Side of the 1983 War Scare," National Security Archive, November 5, 2018.

bases and ports in South Korea, Japan, Guam, and elsewhere.[41] These could be combined with cyber strikes, chemical and biological weapons employment, special operations forces sabotage, and conventional artillery attacks. North Korea's evolving missile force offers it a broad range of potential strike packages, ranging from shorter-range missiles hitting U.S. bases in South Korea to intermediate-range missiles reaching farther out into the Pacific.[42]

Even such a significant attack concept would likely attempt to preserve a residual strategic deterrent (unless U.S. forces were approaching Pyongyang). North Korea's goal might be to have mobile ICBMs and submarine-launched weapons capable of reaching the continental United States as a final deterrent to the United States taking regime-destroying actions.[43]

It is not clear what assumptions North Korea would have to make to assume that strikes of this magnitude could be undertaken without a massive U.S. nuclear counterstrike. DPRK leaders could come to believe that their nuclear threats against the continental United States would deter such a response. They could restrict attacks to U.S. military facilities and hope that this would produce some degree of restraint. The primary motivation, though, might be pure desperation. If North Korea believes that a U.S. campaign to destroy its regime has begun (or is on the verge of beginning), then North Korea might

---

[41] One analysis reviewed DPRK sources for specific potential targets and developed a list that featured Seoul, key bases and port facilities in South Korea (such as Osan, Pyeongtaek, Busan, Gunsan, and Daegu) and locations in Japan, such as Tokyo, Misawa, Yokohama, Yokosuka, Nagoya, Kyoto, and Osaka). See Allard, Duchâtel, and Godement, 2017, pp. 4–5.

[42] Such a strike option could also feature decapitation strikes against ROK political leadership, but such a choice would be highly escalatory and would be more in keeping with a final, all-out act of desperation.

[43] Some DPRK statements have explicitly referred to a two-phase deterrent doctrine. A description of a conflict scenario released by the Korean People's Army in 2016, for example, refers to an initial strike as a "crucial warning" which would be followed by a "second operation to totally eliminate [the enemy] at its source" (Allard, Duchâtel, and Godement, 2017, p. 3).

decide that it has one chance to strike a paralyzing blow, and that the risks involved must be accepted.[44]

As North Korea acquires more capabilities, its doctrine is likely to grow more ambitious for both strategic and bureaucratic reasons. We therefore highlight a third potential for nuclear use which, although not inherent in the default outcome we anticipate, nonetheless must be taken seriously by the United States and its allies. That is the DPRK use of a nuclear umbrella to conduct a regular, volatile series of provocations and small-scale aggressions, perhaps leading gradually to more-elaborate forms of aggression. This scenario envisions regular use of nuclear coercion, including threats of discrete types of nuclear use for leverage purposes (such as demonstration strikes or electromagnetic pulse bursts), in support of gradually more-aggressive DPRK provocations. Even if this did not become established doctrine, it is a pattern of behavior that could emerge in a specific crisis period.[45]

This more offensive concept of nuclear use could eventually reach the ultimate form of coercion: the threat to South Korea to accede to unification under DPRK terms or face annihilation. One DPRK defector, for example, has argued that Kim Jong-Un

> has a kind of illusion that, if he acquires these nuclear weapons and ICBMs, he could be able to compel Washington to pull U.S. troops out of South Korea, and once U.S. troops leave South

---

[44] It should be stressed that a U.S. preemptive strike to take out even part of North Korea's nuclear capacity could lead North Korea to escalate to nuclear use. It could be very difficult, especially given the limits of DPRK political intelligence and operational intelligence, surveillance, and reconnaissance, to distinguish a modest attack from something more elaborate. If a handful of cruise missiles arrived without warning in the absence of any other U.S. military action, the attack might be effectively over before DPRK leadership had time to worry that a more comprehensive U.S. strike was underway. Thus, any significant attack on DPRK facilities, especially C2 sites, risks triggering one of the very few conditions for DPRK nuclear use.

[45] Patrick McEachern has argued that North Korea's nuclear capabilities aim to enhance its overall influence and coercive capabilities (Patrick McEachern, "More Than Regime Survival," *North Korean Review*, Vol. 14, No. 1 Spring 2018).

> Korea, then foreign investments would follow U.S. troops out . . . and . . . then the South Korean business also would leave.[46]

Such claims typically do not reflect direct knowledge of Kim's beliefs, however, and must be treated with at least a modicum of skepticism, partly because such rumors could be deliberately designed to enhance North Korea's ability to engage in coercive diplomacy. Given the broad consensus that North Korea's primary goal is regime survival, there will always be a significant tension between that baseline requirement and any strategy to compel ROK surrender that involves threatening offensive nuclear war against South Korea, which is one of the world's dozen largest economies and a full member of the global democratic community. If any U.S.-ROK alliance remains in place at the time, North Korea would be courting U.S. nuclear annihilation—before it even had a chance to launch its threatened attack. Given potential fallout (nuclear and geopolitical), China would presumably be strongly opposed to such an act, or even the threat of such an attack. Japan, Russia, and others would also stand to be affected; the world community would face a clear example of unprovoked military aggression. Even if its threat worked, North Korea would have to engage in significant amounts of self-delusion to think that it could gain an ROK surrender and join the world community as an accepted, unified Korea. Such wishful thinking is not out of the question, but we have some evidence to believe that Kim and senior DPRK leaders are not completely out of touch with global realities.

In sum, then, evolving DPRK nuclear doctrine and capabilities point to an escalating series of potential cases in which North Korea would cross the threshold to the use of nuclear weapons, outlined in Table 4.3.

An important lesson of this roster of nuclear use scenarios is that the United States and South Korea have a significant ability to control the circumstances that would lead North Korea to undertake nuclear use. The fourth scenario can be forestalled with continuing

---

[46] "North Korean Defector Says Even a Limited Attack by U.S. Would Trigger All-Out War," PBS NewsHour, November 3, 2017.

Table 4.3
Scenarios for DPRK Nuclear Use

Scenario	Forcing Conditions	Form of Nuclear Use
Limited strike to interrupt U.S.-ROK military operations	Conventional fighting underway; U.S.-ROK forces operating inside North Korea or on verge of doing so; no fatal threat to regime yet	Single nuclear warhead or small number of them, likely employed against lead elements of advancing U.S.-ROK forces
Large-scale strike against U.S. force flow and military targets	Conflict might be underway or not yet begun; North Korea perceives that United States is beginning process of large-scale attack to end regime	Dozens of nuclear weapons (the entire DPRK force minus perhaps a handful of strategic-deterrent warheads) delivered against U.S. military facilities and forces; possibly other targets, including ROK and Japanese facilities
Ultimate deterrent strike against U.S. targets	In the endgame, North Korea employs whatever weapons that can reach the territorial United States to punish or paralyze U.S. military action	Small number of ICBM or SLBM weapons targeted against territorial United States
Nuclear coercive threats and potential first strike against South Korea to compel surrender	U.S.-ROK alliance has fractured, China unwilling to prevent outcome, North Korea sees chance to realize its ultimate goal	Unclear; if coercive threat was rejected, could involve a graduated campaign of nuclear use

alliance commitments and coordination with other key actors, including China. The other three would all stem from a DPRK perception of threat to its regime, and in some cases require the initiation of conflict itself. Through a combination of restraint, political agreements to reduce mutual threat perceptions and the perceived risk of war, and continued credible deterrent threats, the United States should be able to have significant confidence in its ability to mitigate the scenarios for DPRK nuclear use.

CHAPTER FIVE

Conclusions

The three discussion papers in this report aim to stimulate policy discussion, research, and information collection on how the DPRK leadership, Kim Jong-Un in particular, makes decisions about North Korea's future. Because there are many gaps in our understanding about Kim's and the leadership's decisionmaking process, the best we can do is outline plausible options that they might consider. Outlining logical pathways, branch points, and options that Kim and his leadership appear likely to consider provides a contextual framework for identifying decisions that lead to courses of action. Being transparent about what we do not know is as important as indicating what we think we know based on the information available. Outlining what is not known with great confidence but seems important provides another field for further data collection and analysis. How Kim, his military leaders, and the DPRK elite cadre sort through options regarding their economy, the military balance on the Korean Peninsula, and the use of nuclear weapons to ensure regime survival will have implications for the Asia-Pacific region broadly defined.

Kim has indicated that "nothing has changed between the day when we maintained the line of simultaneously pushing forward the economic construction and the building of nuclear force."[1] If the economic improvement embarked on without significant sanctions relief is confined to showcase tourist resort projects, the case studies in this

1 "Report of the Fifth Plenary Meeting of 7th Central Committee of the WPK (Kim Jong Un's 2020 New Year Address)," as published and translated into English by the Korean Central News Agency, National Committee of North Korea, January 1, 2020.

report indicate that it is unlikely that North Korea will meaningfully open markets and engage the global economy, as China and Vietnam did in the previous four decades. Tourism is an area less affected by international sanctions. Building showcase tourist resorts in SEZs away from the general population can be structured such that an elite cadre receives the greatest benefits. However, evidence of economic projects other than tourist resorts in SEZs might signal a desire to embrace open market opportunities and engage in commerce with foreign entities.

Military stability on the Korean Peninsula is in the interest of North and South Korea, the United States, and other powers in the Asia-Pacific region. As the two scenarios in the second paper in this report illustrate, if conventional deterrence breaks down, there are few ways to prevent escalation to greater levels of high-intensity violence. As a result, all parties should be careful to not test the integrity of conventional military deterrence.

A catalytic triggering event seems necessary to erode the integrity of conventional deterrence on the Korean Peninsula. As illustrated in the scenarios considered in this report, unexpected events stemming from such mistakes as the downing of a passenger airliner or a misinterpreted move to overthrow the regime in North Korea could easily lead to strategic tragedy. Changes in ROK defense policy and the U.S.-ROK relationship are important contextual factors that might influence the military balance on the Peninsula. South Korean President Moon's administration policy changes for ROK military posture that focus on other regional threats could change DPRK perceptions of the strength of the ROK military. Over a longer period, declining ROK birth rates could lead to a smaller available population to fill the military ranks. Monitoring Kim and the DPRK leadership's reactions to these issues might provide insight into their perception of the stability of the conventional military balance on the Peninsula. If Kim and DPRK leaders do not perceive these issues as eroding ROK and U.S. conventional military capabilities, then—barring a catastrophic event that threatens North Korea in some fashion—deterrence on the Peninsula probably would remain stable. In themselves, these contextual factors do not seem sufficient at this point to embolden North Korea to take unprovoked and risky offensive military moves.

But an unexpected event that North Korea perceives as threatening combined with a series of changes that shift ROK military agility could undermine strategic stability on the Korean Peninsula. Developments that make strategic stability brittle raise the possibility of North Korea wielding nuclear weapons in ways to ensure regime survival. Because a security or nonintervention guarantee from the United States is neither likely nor credible to the North Koreans, the Kim regime will likely continue to slowly modernize the country's capability over time. It is safe to infer that North Korea's nuclear arsenal size and targeting doctrine is designed to provide enough of a deterrent posture to guarantee regime survival.

In many ways, North Korea has become an unrecognized nuclear power like Pakistan and India. Nuclear weapons provide for regime survival, and that is Kim's desired purpose. North Korea's 2013 law on nuclear weapons is the most concrete indication of the regime's thinking about the use of nuclear weapons. Of note is how this law casts nuclear weapons as defensive in nature. The U.S. military footprint in the region is large and recognizable, and any significant U.S. military moves to ready follow-on forces in Japan or evacuate civilian dependents will likely spook the DPRK regime. Any movements that appear to be a prelude to war might trigger rash action on the part of North Korea. Given the scarcity of information, it is very difficult to render a firm judgment about how Kim and other DPRK leaders consider their options for using nuclear weapons.

The United States is fortunate to control some of the variables that might influence North Korea's nuclear-use calculations. As noted at the end of Chapter Four, a combination of measures will reduce the risk and the United States can exercise them alone, with South Korea, with nations involved in the six party talks, and/or with the United Nations Security Council. Political negotiations that lead to agreements can reduce mutual threat perceptions and increase an understanding of the risk of war. As all sides seek political agreements, maintaining credible conventional and nuclear deterrents will be important. Monitoring North Korea's interests in political agreements and its appreciation of deterrence can inform policymakers about which political engagements are important. This combination of measures can mitigate the prospect of DPRK nuclear use. Stability over time affords opportunities for all parties to change in ways that make conflict less likely.

References

"2013 Plenary Meeting of WPK Central Committee and 7th Session of Supreme People's Assembly," North Korean Economy Watch, April 1, 2013. As of June 20, 2020:
https://www.nkeconwatch.com/2013/04/01/2013-plenary-meeting-of-wpk-central-committee-and-supreme-peoples-assembly/

"7th PCC Central Report, Presented by First Secretary Raúl Castro Ruz," transcript, CubaDebate, April 18, 2016.

Allard, Léonie, Mathieu Duchâtel, and François Godement, *Pre-Empting Defeat: In Search of North Korea's Nuclear Doctrine*, London: European Council on Foreign Relations, November 22, 2017. As of June 15, 2020:
https://www.ecfr.eu/publications/summary/pre_empting_defeat_in_search_of_north_koreas_nuclear_doctrine

Appleman, Roy E., *South to the Naktong, North to the Yalu*, June 1950–November 1950, Washington, D.C.: Center of Military History, 1961.

Banco Central de Cuba, *Cuba's Banking and Financial System*, 2nd ed., 1998.

Bechtol, Bruce, "Planning for the Unthinkable: Countering a North Korean Nuclear Attack and Management of Post-Attack Scenarios," *Korean Journal of Defense Analysis*, Vol. 23, No. 1, March 2011, pp. 1–17.

Beresford, Melanie, *National Unification and Economic Development in Vietnam*, Basingstoke, UK: MacMillan, 1989a.

———, "Vietnam Socialist Agriculture in Transition," *Journal of Contemporary Asia*, Vol. 24, No. 4, 1989b, pp. 466–486.

Bermudez, Joseph S., Jr., *North Korea's Development of a Nuclear Weapons Strategy*, Washington, D.C.: U.S.-Korea Institute at Johns Hopkins School of Advanced International Studies, 2015.

Buzo, Adrian, *Politics and Leadership in North Korea*, 2nd ed., New York: Routledge, 2017.

Canh, Nguyen Van, *Vietnam Under Communism, 1975–1982*, Stanford, Calif.: Stanford University, Hoover Institution Press, 2017.

Cha, Victor, "North Korea's Weapons of Mass Destruction," *Political Science Quarterly*, Vol. 117, No. 2, Summer 2002, pp. 209–230.

Cho, B. H., *North Korea's Special Economic Zone Development Trend and Inter-Korean Cooperation* (북한의 경제특구 개발 동향과 남북협력 연계방안), Seoul: Korea Development Institute, September 2014.

Choi Ik-Jae (최익재), "Kim Jong-Un Demands Xi Jinping to Negotiate with Four North Korean Bases (김정은, 시진핑에 북한 4대 거점 경협 요구)," *JoongAng Ilbo* (중앙일보), June 6, 2018. As of June 16, 2020:
https://news.joins.com/article/22689717

Cormaic, Ruadhán Mac, "Cardinal's Secret U.S. Visit Paved Way for Obama-Castro Détente," *Irish Times*, March 16, 2017. As of June 20, 2020:
https://www.irishtimes.com/news/world/cardinal-s-secret-us-visit-paved-way-for-obama-castro-détente-1.3011667

Council on Hemispheric Affairs, "The European Union and Cuba: The Common Position," July 15, 2010. As of June 15, 2020:
http://www.coha.org/the-european-union-and-cuba-the-common-position/

Creamer, Shawn Patrick, "The United Nations Command and Sending States," unpublished monograph, undated. As of June 15, 2020:
http://icks.org/n/data/ijks/2017FW-4.pdf

———, *Answering the Korea Question: U.S. Government Policy Toward the Unified Command and the Korean Armistice Agreement*, Carlisle, Pa.: U.S. Army War College, Civilian Research Project, March 2017.

Dollar, David, "The Hanoi Summit Shines a Light on the 'Vietnam Model' of Development," Brookings Institution, February 27, 2019. As of March 25, 2019:
https://www.brookings.edu/blog/order-from-chaos/2019/02/27/the-hanoi-summit-shines-a-light-on-the-vietnam-model-of-development/

Duiker, William J., "Ideology and Nation-Building in the Democratic Republic of Vietnam," *Asian Survey*, Vol. 17, No. 5, May 1977, pp. 413–431.

Ebashi, Masahiko, "The Economic Takeoff," in James W. Morley and Masashi Nishihara, eds., *Vietnam Joins the World*, New York: M. E. Sharpe, 1997.

Feinberg, Richard E., *Open for Business: Building the New Cuban Economy*, Washington, D.C.: Brookings Institution Press, 2016.

Fewsmith, Joseph, *Dilemmas of Reform in China: Political Conflict and Economic Debate*, Armonk, N.Y.: M. E. Sharpe, 1994.

Fforde, Adam, "Review of *Profit and Poverty in Rural Vietnam: Winners and Losers of a Dismantled Revolution*" (by Rita Liljestrom, Eva Lindskog, Nguyen Van Anh, and Vuong Xuan Tinh), *Journal of Asian Studies*, Vol. 58, No. 3, 1999, pp. 898–899.

Fforde, Adam, and Stefan deVylder, *From Plan to Market: The Economic Transition in Vietnam*, Boulder, Colo.: Westview Press, 1996.

Fifield, Anna, "North Korea's One-Percenters Savor Life in 'Pyonghattan,'" *Washington Post*, May 14, 2016.

Gentile, Gian, Yvonne K. Crane, Dan Madden, Timothy M. Bonds, Bruce W. Bennett, Michael J. Mazarr, and Andrew Scobell, *Four Problems on the Korean Peninsula: North Korea's Expanding Nuclear Capabilities Drive a Complex Set of Problems*, Santa Monica, Calif.: RAND Corporation, TL-271-A, 2019. As of June 15, 2020:
https://www.rand.org/pubs/tools/TL271.html

Gonzalez, Edward, and David Ronfeldt, *Cuba Adrift in a Postcommunist World*, Santa Monica, Calif.: RAND Corporation, R-4231-USDP, 1992. As of June 15, 2020:
https://www.rand.org/pubs/reports/R4231.html

———, *Storm Warnings for Cuba*, Santa Monica, Calif.: RAND Corporation, MR-452-OSD, 1994. As of June 15, 2020:
https://www.rand.org/pubs/monograph_reports/MR452.html

Gordon, Michael R., and Andrew Jeong, "Kim Jong Un Extends Peace Overture to U.S.," *Wall Street Journal*, January 1, 2019.

Haggard, Stephan M., and Marcus Noland, "North Korea's External Economic Relations," Peterson Institute of International Economics Working Paper No. 07-7, August 2007.

Hale, Christopher D., "Real Reform in North Korea? The Aftermath of the July 2002 Economic Measures," *Asian Survey*, Vol. 45, No. 6, 2005, pp. 823–842.

Halperin, Morton, Peter Hayes, Thomas Pickering, Leon Sigal, and Philip Yun, "From Enemies to Security Partners: Pathways to Denuclearization in Korea," Nautilus Peace and Security Network Net Policy Forum, July 6, 2018.

Hare, Paul, "North Korea: Building the Institutions to Raise Living Standards," *International Economic Journal*, Vol. 26, No. 3, September 2012, pp 487–509.

Hayes, Peter, and Scott Bruce, "Translating North Korea's Nuclear Threats into Constrained Operational Reality," in Gregory Moore, ed., *North Korean Nuclear Operationality*, Baltimore, Md.: Johns Hopkins University Press, 2014, pp. 15–31.

Hayes, Peter, and Roger Cavazos, "North Korea in 2014: A Fresh Leap Forward Into Thin Air?" *Asian Survey*, Vol. 55, No. 1, January/February 2015, pp. 119–131.

Hermes, Walter G., *Truce Tent to Fighting Front*, Washington, D.C.: Center of Military History, 1966.

Herskowitz, Jon, and Kim Junghyun, "South Korean Tourist Shot Dead by North Soldier," Reuters, July 11, 2008.

Hiep, Le Hong, "Vietnam's Domestic-Foreign Policy Nexus: *Doi Moi*, Foreign Policy Reform, and Sino-Vietnamese Normalization," *Asian Politics & Policy*, Vol. 5, No. 3, June 25, 2013.

———, *Living Next to the Giant: The Political Economy of Vietnam's Relations with China Under Doi Moi*, Institute of Southeast Asian Studies–Yusof Ishak Institute, 2017. As of September 28, 2017:
https://bookshop.iseas.edu.sg/publication/2201

———, "The Vietnam Model for North Korea," *Project Syndicate*, February 26, 2019. As of March 25, 2019:
https://www.project-syndicate.org/commentary/trump-kim-summit-north-korea-reforms-by-le-hong-hiep-2019-02

Hong, J. H., *North Korean Economy in the Kim Jong-Un Regime for 5 Years: Focusing on Economic Policy* (김정은 정권 5년의 북한경제: 경제정책을 중심으로), Seoul: Korea Institute for National Unification, 2017.

Huong Le Thu, "Can Vietnam's Doi Moi Reforms Be an Inspiration for North Korea?" ASAN Forum, August 23, 2018. As of March 25, 2019:
http://www.theasanforum.org/can-vietnams-doi-moi-reforms-be-an-inspiration-for-north-korea/

Information Office of the State Council, *China's Foreign Trade*, Beijing, December 2011.

"Interfering with Various Interests of the North Korean Version of the 'President' and Taking Bribes (북한판 '태자당' 각종 이권 개입하며 뇌물 받아)," Voice of America (미국의 소리), December 1, 2010. As of June 15, 2020:
https://www.voakorea.com/a/nk-corruption-111141629/1337652.html

Jones, Nate, "The Soviet Side of the 1983 War Scare," National Security Archive, November 5, 2018. As of June 15, 2020:
https://nsarchive.gwu.edu/briefing-book/aa83/2018-11-05/soviet-side-1983-war-scare

Joung, Eun-Lee, "North Korea's Economic Policy as a Duet with Control and Relaxation: Dynamics Arising from the Development of Public Markets Since the North Korean Famines in the 1990s," *Journal of Asian Public Policy*, Vol. 9, No. 1, 2016, pp. 75–94.

Kaesong Industrial District Management Committee, homepage, undated. As of June 15, 2020:
https://www.kidmac.or.kr

"Kaesong Talks: North and South Korea Reach Agreement," BBC, July 7, 2013. As of June 15, 2020:
https://www.bbc.com/news/world-asia-23208617

KCNA—*See* Korean Central News Agency.

Khan, Zafar, *Pakistan's Nuclear Policy: A Minimum Credible Deterrence*, Abingdon, UK: Routledge, 2015.

Kim Da-Hye (김다혜), "Kim Jong-Un Visited Pyeongbuk-Sindo-Gun on the Border with China (김정은 방중 후 첫 행보는 중국접경 평북 신도군 시찰)," News1, June 30, 2018. As of June 15, 2020:
http://news1.kr/articles/?3359373

Kim, Sung Chull, "North Korea's Nuclear Doctrine and Revisionist Strategy," in Sung Chull Kim and Michael D. Cohen, *North Korea and Nuclear Weapons: Entering the New Era of Deterrence*, Washington, D.C.: Georgetown University Press, 2017, pp. 31–54.

Kim, Y. H., "Kim Jong-Un Administration's Economic Reform Evaluation for the Second Year in Power (집권 2년차, 김정은 정권의 경제개혁 평가)," *KDI North Korea Economic Review* (KDI 북한경제리뷰), March 2014, pp. 25–38.

Kong, Tat Yan, "The Political Obstacles to Economic Reform in North Korea: The Ultra Cautious Strategy in Comparative Perspective," *Pacific Review*, Vol. 27, No. 1, 2014, pp. 73–96.

Korean Central News Agency, "KCNA Report on a Successful 3rd Underground Nuclear Test," February 12, 2013a.

———, "Law on Consolidating Position of Nuclear Weapons State Adopted," April 1, 2013b.

———, "Official Statement of the National Emergency Measures Committee on Opposition Against Nuclear War Exercises to Invade DPRK," April 23, 2015a.

———, "Official Statement of the Committee for the Peaceful Reunification of Korea," August 12, 2015b.

———, "Question and Answer with President of Nuclear Scientific Research Center," September 15, 2015c.

———, "Crucial Statement of KPA Supreme Command," February 23, 2016a.

———, "Kim Jong Un Guides Drill for Ballistic Rocket Fire, "July 20, 2016b.

Kwang, Sub Kwak, *The US-ROK Alliance, 1953–2001, Alliance Institutionalization*, Ann Arbor, Mich.: Michigan University Press, 2006.

Lankov, Andrei, "North Korea's Nuclear Blackmail," *New York Times*, opinion piece, November 25, 2010.

———, *The Resurgence of a Market Economy in North Korea*, Moscow: Carnegie Moscow Center, 2016.

———, "The New Leader, The New Economic Model," in William H. Overholt, ed., *North Korea: Peace? Nuclear War?* Cambridge, Mass.: Mossavar-Rahmani Center for Business and Government, 2019, pp. 97–111.

Lee, Chung H., "A Study of the DPRK's Economic Policy Through the Seventh Party Convention" (in Korean), *Review of North Korean Studies*, Vol. 19, No. 3, 2016, pp. 94–154.

Lee, Hong Yung, "North Korea in 2013: Economy, Executions, and Nuclear Brinkmanship," *Asian Survey*, Vol. 54, No. 1, January/February 2014, pp. 89–100.

Lee, Jong-Wha, and Ju Hyun Pyun, "North Korea's Economic Integration and Growth Potential," *Asian Economic Journal*, Vol. 32, No. 3, September 2018, pp. 301–325.

Lee, Keun, Byung-Yeon Kim, and Insook Lee, "The Possibility of Economic Reform in North Korea," *Journal of Contemporary Asia*, Vol. 39, No. 2, May 2009, pp. 279–294.

Lewis, Jeffrey, *The 2020 Commission Report on the North Korean Nuclear Attacks Against the United States: A Speculative Novel*, New York: Mariner Books, 2018.

Lieber, Keir A., and Daryl G. Press, *Coercive Nuclear Campaigns in the 21st Century: Understanding Adversary Incentives and Options for Nuclear Escalation*, Monterey, Calif.: U.S. Naval Postgraduate School, Report 2013-001, March 2013.

Lim, Jae-Cheon, "Institutional Change in North Korean Economic Development Since 1984: The Competition Between Hegemonic and Non-Hegemonic Rules and Norms," *Pacific Affairs*, Vol. 82, No. 1, Spring 2009, pp. 9–27.

London, Jonathan, "Viet Nam and the Making of Market-Leninism," *Pacific Review*, Vol. 22, No. 3, July 2009, pp. 375–399. As of March 27, 2019: https://www.tandfonline.com/doi/pdf/10.1080/09512740903068404?needAccess=true

Mansourov, Alexandre Y., "The Origins, Evolution, and Current Politics of the North Korean Nuclear Program," *Nonproliferation Review*, Spring-Summer 1995, pp. 25–38.

———, "North Korea: The Dramatic Fall of Jang Song Thaek," *38 North*, December 9, 2013.

———, *Kim Jong Un's Nuclear Doctrine and Strategy: What Everyone Needs to Know*, Berkeley, Calif.: Nautilus Institute for Security and Sustainability, Nautilus Peace and Security Special Reports, December 16, 2014. As of June 15, 2020: https://nautilus.org/napsnet/napsnet-special-reports/kim-jong-uns-nuclear-doctrine-and-strategy-what-everyone-needs-to-know/

Matray, James I., "Korea's War at 60: A Survey of the Literature," *Cold War History*, Vol. 11, No. 1, February 2011, pp. 99–129.

McEachern, Patrick, "More Than Regime Survival," *North Korean Review*, Vol. 14, No. 1, Spring 2018, pp. 115–118.

Meisner, Maurice, *The Deng Xiaoping Era: An Inquiry into the Fate of Chinese Socialism, 1978–1994*, New York: Hill and Wang, 1996.

Mesa-Lago, Carmelo, "The Emerging Non-State Sector in Cuba's Economy," *Latin American Research Review*, Vol. 52, No. 1, July 2017, pp. 150–156.

Meyerle, Jerry, *Nuclear Weapons and Coercive Escalation in Regional Conflicts: Lessons from North Korea and Pakistan*, Arlington, Va.: CNA, November 2014.

Mikelionis, Lukas, "North Korea's Top Diplomat in Italy Defected, Embarrassing Kim Jong Un," Fox News, January 3, 2019.

Millet, Allan R., *The War For Korea: They Came from the North*, Lawrence, Kan.: University Press of Kansas, 2010.

Minich, James M., *The North Korean's People's Army: Origins and Current Tactics*, Annapolis, Md.: Naval Institute Press, 2005.

Mujal-León, Eusebio, "Survival, Adaptation and Uncertainty: The Case of Cuba," *Journal of International Affairs*, Vol. 65, No. 1, Fall/Winter 2011, pp. 149–168.

"N. Korea Withdraws Demand for Steep Wage Hike at Joint Park," Yonhap News Agency, September 11, 2009. As of June 15, 2020: https://en.yna.co.kr/view/AEN20090911002700315

"N. Korean, Hong Kong Firms to Develop Border City of Sinuiju," Yonhap News Agency, March 12, 2014. As of June 15, 2020: https://en.yna.co.kr/view/AEN20140312004800315

Nakazawa, Katsuji, "Chinese Billionaire Who Plotted with North Korea Pops Up After 16 Years," *Nikkei Asian Review*, October 25, 2018. As of June 16, 2020: https://asia.nikkei.com/Editor-s-Picks/China-up-close/Chinese-billionaire-who-plotted-with-North-Korea-pops-up-after-16-years

Nam, Phan Doan, "Ngoai giao Viet Nam sau 20 nam doi moi [Vietnam's Diplomacy After 20 Years]," *Tap Chi Cong San [Communist Review]*, July 14, 2006.

Narang, Vipin, "Nuclear Strategies of Emerging Nuclear Powers: North Korea and Iran," *Washington Quarterly*, Vol. 38, No. 1, Spring 2015, pp. 73–91.

———, "Why Kim Jong-un Wouldn't Be Irrational to Use a Nuclear Weapon First," *Washington Post*, September 8, 2017.

Natsios, Andrew S., *The Great North Korean Famine: Famine, Politics, and Foreign Policy*, Washington, D.C.: U.S. Institute of Peace Press, 2001.

Naughton, Barry, *Growing Out of the Plan: Chinese Economic Reform 1978–1993*, New York: Cambridge University Press, 1996.

Nguyen Manh Hung, "Thuc hien nhat quan dong loi doi ngoai doc lap, tu chu, hoa binh, hop tac va phat trien [Consistently Implementing the Foreign Policy of Independence, Autonomy, Peace, and Development]," *Tap Chi Cong San* [*Communist Review*], September 17, 2006.

"North Korea's Central Broadcaster: 'Kim Jong-Un Inspects Sinuiju and Maps Construction Plans' (북한 중앙방송 "김정은, 신의주 시찰하고 건설계획 지도)," Maekyung Economics, November 16, 2018. As of June 15, 2020: https://www.mk.co.kr/news/politics/view/2018/11/718593/

"North Korean Defector Says Even a Limited Attack by U.S. Would Trigger All-Out War," PBS NewsHour, November 3, 2017. As of June 15, 2020: https://www.pbs.org/newshour/show/north-korean-defector-says-even-a-limited-attack-by-u-s-would-trigger-all-out-war

O'Neil, Andrew, "North Korea's Changing Nuclear Posture," *The Strategist*, April 17, 2013.

Pearson, James, and Ju-min Park, "The War That Never Ends Between the Koreas," Reuters, June 16, 2014. As of March 16, 2020: https://www.reuters.com/article/us-northkorea-islands-insight/the-war-that-never-ends-between-the-koreas-idUSKBN0ES00720140617

Pollack, Jonathan D., *The Sino-Soviet Rivalry and Chinese Security Debate*, Santa Monica, Calif.: RAND Corporation, R-2907-AF, 1982. As of June 8, 2020: https://www.rand.org/pubs/reports/R2907.html

Public Law 106-387, Agriculture, Rural Development, Food and Drug Administration Appropriations Act, October 28, 2000.

Public Law 111-8, Omnibus Appropriations Act, March 11, 2009.

Quan Hoang Vuong, "Vietnam's Political Economy in Transition (1986–2016)," *Stratfor*, May 27, 2014. As of March 28, 2019: https://worldview.stratfor.com/article/vietnams-political-economy-transition-1986-2016

Quan Hoang Vuong, Dam Van Nhue, Daniel van Houtte, and Tri Dung Tran, "The Entrepreneurial Facets as Precursor to Vietnam's Economic Renovation in 1986," *IUP Journal of Entrepreneurship Development*, Vol. VIII, No. 4, December 2011, pp. 6–47. As of March 26, 2019: https://papers.ssrn.com/sol3/papers.cfm?abstract_id=2141196

"Report of the Fifth Plenary Meeting of the 7th Central Committee of the WPK (Kim Jong Un's 2020 New Year Address)," *as published and translated into English by the Korean Central News Agency,* National Committee of North Korea, January 1, 2020. As of February 25, 2020: https://www.ncnk.org/resources/publications/kju_2020_new_years_plenum_report.pdf/file_view

Republic of Korea, *2016 Defense White Paper*, Seoul: Ministry of National Defense, May 2017.

Roehrig, Terrence, *North Korea's Nuclear Weapons: Future Strategy and Doctrine*, Cambridge, Mass.: Harvard University Kennedy School, Belfer Center, May 2013.

Rosone, James, and Miranda Watson, *Battlefield Korea*, Book Two of the Red Storm Rising Series, Grand Rapids, Mich.: Front Line Publishing, 2017.

Ryall, Julian, "North Korea Recalls Diplomats to Undergo 'Ideological Examinations' After Embarrassing Defections," *The Telegraph*, March 29, 2019.

Sanford, John M., and Andrew Scobell, *North Korea's Military Threat: Pyongyang's Conventional Forces, Weapons of Mass Destruction, and Ballistic Missiles*, Carlisle, Pa.: Strategic Studies Institute Publications, April 3, 2020. As of June 20, 2020: https://ssi.armywarcollege.edu/north-koreas-military-threat-pyongyangs-conventional-forces-weapons-of-mass-destruction-and-ballistic-missiles

Schnabel, James F., and Robert J. Watson, *History of the Joint Chiefs of Staff*, Vol. III, *The Joint Chiefs of Staff and National Policy, 1950–1951, The Korean War, Part 1*, Washington, D.C.: Office of Joint History, Office of the Chairman of the Joint Chiefs of Staff, 1998.

Schuler, Paul, and Mai Truong, "Leadership Reshuffle and the Future of Vietnam's Collective Leadership," *Perspective*, Vol. 2019, No. 9, ISEAS Yusof Ishak Institute, February 22, 2019. As of March 26, 2019: https://www.iseas.edu.sg/images/pdf/ISEAS_Perspective_2019_9.pdf.

Sechser, Todd S., and Matthew Fuhrmann, "The Coercive Limits of Nuclear Weapons," paper prepared for the Annual Meeting of the International Studies Association, Montreal, Canada, March 16–19, 2011.

Seelye, Katharine Q., "Cardinal Jaime Ortega, a Cuban Bridge to the U.S., Dies at 82," *New York Times*, July 26, 2019. As of June 22, 2020: https://www.nytimes.com/2019/07/26/world/americas/cardinal-jaime-ortega-dead.html

Sharif, Naubahar, and Mitchell M. Tseng, "The Role of Hong Kong in Mainland China's Modernization in Manufacturing," *Asian Survey*, Vol. 51, No. 4, July/August 2011, pp. 633–658.

Shorrock, Tim, "Can the United Nations Command Become a Catalyst for Change on the Korean Peninsula?" *National Interest*, November 1, 2018.

Smith, Josh, "Buying a Big Stick: South Korea's Military Spending Has North Korea Worried," Reuters, September 10, 2019.

Song Sang-ho, "Defense Reform Plan to Cut Generals, Create Ground Command, Retain 3-Axis System," Yonhap News Agency, July 27, 2019.

Stainback, Grace, "Exploring the Cultural and Infrastructural Impacts of Consumerism on the New Cuba," *Hatfield Graduate Journal of Public Affairs*, Vol. 3, No. 1, 2018, pp. 1–19.

Stanton, Joshua, "The 'Experts' Were Wrong. The Sanctions Are Working," *Free Korea*, April 23, 2019.

Sun, Yan, *The Chinese Reassessment of Socialism, 1976–1992*, Princeton, N.J.: Princeton University Press, 1995.

Sungyoung Jang, "How Will 'Defense Reform 2.0' Change South Korea's Defense?" *The Diplomat*, August 27, 2018.

Thang, Bui Tat, "After the War: 25 Years of Economic Development in Vietnam," (commentary), *NIRA Review*, Tokyo: National Institute for Research Advancement, Spring 2000, pp. 21–25. As of March 28, 2019: http://www.nira.or.jp/past/publ/review/2000spring/06thang.pdf

Thayer, Carlyle A., "Vietnam's Foreign Policy in an Era of Rising Sino-U.S. Competition: Providing Equity to the Major Powers While Pursuing Proactive International Integration," presentation to Conference on Great Power Rivalries, Domestic Politics, and Southeast Asian Foreign Policy, The Dorothy Borg Research Project, Weatherhead East Asia Institute, Columbia University, November 10–11, 2016. As of September 27, 2017: http://viet-studies.net/kinhte/VNForeignPolicy_Thayer.pdf

———, "Vietnam's Foreign Policy in an Era of Rising Sino-U.S. Competition and Increasing Domestic Political Influence," *Asian Security*, Vol. 13, No. 3, July 31, 2017, pp. 183–199. As of March 25, 2019: http://www.tandfonline.com/doi/full/10.1080/14799855.2017.1354570?src=recsys

"Total Trade," North Korea in the World, webpage, undated. As of April 9, 2019: https://www.northkoreaintheworld.org/economic/total-merchandise-trade

Trump, Donald J., and Kim Jong-Un, joint statement, Singapore Summit, June 12, 2018. As of March 17, 2020: https://www.whitehouse.gov/briefings-statements/joint-statement-president-donald-j-trump-united-states-america-chairman-kim-jong-un-democratic-peoples-republic-korea-singapore-summit/

Tung Nguyen Vu, "Chapter 8: Vietnam's Security Challenges: Hanoi's New Approach to National Security and Implications to Defense and Foreign Policies," in National Institute for Defense Studies, *Asia Pacific Countries' Security Outlook and its Implications for the Defense Sector*, Tokyo, NIDS Joint Research Series No. 5, 2010, pp. 107–122. As of September 28, 2017: http://www.nids.mod.go.jp/english/publication/joint_research/series5/pdf/5-8.pdf

Van Diepen, Vann H., and Daniel R. Depetris, "Putting North Korea's New Short-Range Missiles into Perspective," *38 North*, September 5, 2019.

Vu Tuan Anh, ed., *Vietnam's Economic Reform: Results and Problems*, Hanoi: Social Science Publishing House, 1994. As of March 27, 2019: https://idl-bnc-idrc.dspacedirect.org/bitstream/handle/10625/15414/102742.pdf?sequence=1

Wertz, Daniel, Matthew McGrath, and Scott LaFoy, "North Korea's Nuclear Weapons Program," National Committee on North Korea, April 2018. As of June 15, 2020:
https://www.ncnk.org/resources/publications/DPRK-Nuclear-Weapons-Issue-Brief.pdf

World Bank, "The World Bank in Vietnam: Overview," October 5, 2018. As of March 25, 2019:
https://www.worldbank.org/en/country/vietnam/overview

Yeo Jun-suk, "Moon Administration Seeks to Cut Service Period to 18 Months," *Korea Herald*, May 3, 2018. As of June 16, 2020:
http://www.koreaherald.com/view.php?ud=20180503000809

Yonhap News Agency, "S. Korean Firms in Gaeseong Complex Plagued by North's Hefty Taxes," *Korea Times*, October 18, 2012. As of June 15, 2020:
http://www.koreatimes.co.kr/www/news/nation/2012/10/120_122538.html

Youngnam, Kim, "N. Korean Debt to Sweden Remains Unpaid After Four Decades," Voice of America, October 26, 2017.

Zhou, Kate Xiao, *How the Farmers Changed China: Power of the People*, New York: WestView Press, 1996.